We Ploughed By Moonlight

Ethel Fisher M.B.E.

HILLS BOOKS

First Print: October 2001

ISBN: 0952681463

Published by:
Hills Books
Lowther Road
Clay Flatts Estate
Workington
Cumbria
CA14 2DR

Printed by Lintons Printers, County Durham.

THE BENSON FAMILY

This book is dedicated to our family,
and others who farmed, when horse-power ruled the world.

Contents

Introduction

"To plough to sow, to reap and mow
- to be a farmer's boy!"

This song was very popular when I was a child, despite it being every small boy's ambition to be an engine driver. I myself had no choice in the matter, being born into a farming family, like my Father and Grandfather before me, I was hired from the first day I drew breath, and never regretted it.

In the following pages, I have tried to portray a bird's eye view of what life was like, living on a farm sixty years ago, when I knew far more about thinning turnips and feeding calves, than I did of history and arithmetic, looking upon school attendance as a sheer waste of valuable time.

However, despite all the hard work entailed, we also had our 'merry moments' many of which are described within these pages, such as the sheepdog who didn't pay his busfare, the real Halloween Ghost, the drunken farm cyclist, and many others including "Why did the jockey wear brass-nebbed clogs?" "What wakened the tramp, as he slept in the byre?" "Who was the sixpenny man?" "Why did the ponies wear a blindfold?" And "What home-truth did the farmer tell his parish vicar?"

To find the answers, - read on

Our Farm

St Helen's Farm was situated in an odd position, which Dad often described as being "No Man' s Land". We were residents of Seaton Parish, our postal address was Flimby, Holy Trinity at Northside our parish church, St Peters Camerton our burial ground, and Flimby Council School our education centre. Despite this, it was a very interesting place to live, and we enjoyed life.

St. Helens Colliery Brickworks erected 1902, ceased working in 1912 and demolished in 1961.

The farm consisted of five hundred acres of arable and pastureland, all in a ring fence, which meant that no other farmer had any fields within our boundaries. The farm belonged to St Helen's Colliery Co, which was then owned by Sir Samuel Kelly. Both Granda and Dad, in turn, were farm managers, and John Alfred Cape of "Seaton Villa" was the overseer, who visited us every Tuesday morning, in one of the very few motor-cars which were around at the time, it's registration number being AAO 114 - funny how little details stick in one's mind.

At one time, many years ago, there had been a colliery situated on the same site, which was called St Helen's Colliery - not to be confused with the colliery at Siddick, which adopted the same name. There was a St Helen's Brickworks here too, and because of these industries, many old

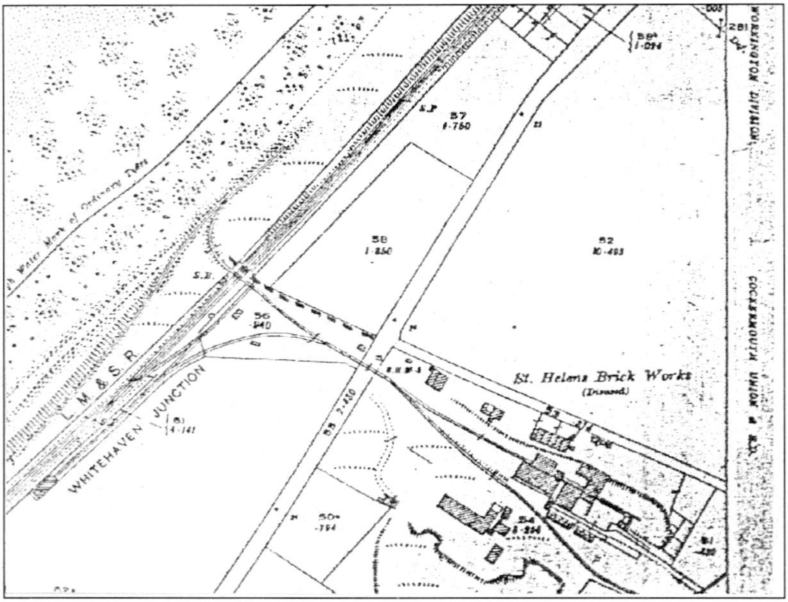

Map showing railway crossing main road and Maryport to Workington Railway at St. Helen's Brickworks

reminders were still in existence, such as the "Lamp Cabin", - a red brick circular building, with stunning arched windows, where the swallows nested, and a stone built powder house, which had double thickness walls, but the most prominent feature of all, were the two gigantic, very tall chimneys, which dominated the skyline. I can well remember these being demolished while I was a schoolgirl, - the sight of them toppling over will be forever etched in my mind.

A railway line was laid from the colliery, crossing the Workington to Maryport main trunk road, before it crossed the Carlisle to Barrow railway line, then carried on along the shores of the Solway Firth, to Siddick. Two large signal boxes, and a big engine shed, built of red brick, again with the lovely arched windows, housed the 'donkey engines' used for hauling the coal, but these had ceased to function while I was a small child, and I cannot recall seeing them. The relics left behind, were still in evidence during the 1930-40 years, and all added to the interest of living at the farm, especially when the old defunct mine-shaft overflowed and as children, we taught ourselves to build some super dams, despite Dad's oft repeated warnings, to "keep away".

Because of the farm's situation, many of our fields had names relating to the old colliery, such as Pitfield, Airshaft field, and Powder House field. Every other field had it's own name, including Stackyard Blinndy, Pinfold, and the Clay Dubs field, which had been the place from where the clay was taken, for the Brickworks.

During the second world war, one of our larger fields had a mock factory built in it, and in another field approx. half a mile away, was a dug-out, which was underground, and consisted of two small rooms. One was furnished with a bench and two stools, while the other housed a quantity of electrical equipment. If an air-raid siren sounded, switches were pulled down, within the dug-out, and the mock factory a few fields away became lit up. This was to detract enemy planes from the Mossbay Steelworks, and Workington Docks. The 'station' was manned mainly by disabled exservicemen, who spent quite a bit of time with us, on the farm, and were a great help during haytime and harvest.

Another wartime memory entails the day two low-flying Spitfires were over our Stackyard field, when one suddenly nose-dived and landed in the gateway, with it's tail sticking up in the air. The pilot wasn't badly

St. Helens Farmyard

hurt, and the other plane landed safely in the same field. Ten soldiers were sent from the army camp at Carlisle. To guard the stricken plane and they all lodged with us, on the farm. This made a lot of extra work, but was very worthwhile, as an army lorry arrived, full of extra rations, and what a beano we had! I remember they left about twenty tins of Spam behind, among other things. They stayed ten days, then a transporter arrived from Silloth airfield, to remove the damaged plane, and the soldiers had to return to Carlisle, but not before we organized a party, and had a good old sing-song round the piano, then they were gone, and the Stackyard field was once more free of sightseers.

Another field contained large ponds, where swans and many other water birds nested, - this area is now a nature reserve. Closer to home, was a range of old pit banks, which added to our playground, where, as children, we could slide down these banks, sitting in old tin sheep troughs, providing great fun, and a sense of achievement, if we won the race to the bottom!

Joiner's shop gang at Old St. Helens Colliery (not Siddick).
St. Helens Farm in background

Apart from all this, we had a very large homestead, consisting of the farmhouse, with it's near-by dairy and cooling house, stables for ten horses, various sized 'loose boxes' pig styes, calf pens, poultry hulls, turnip house, tatie house, cart shed, granary and several cow byres, plus a large enclosed stall, always called "the hospital" which was used to house any animal needing extra care. Our five large barns were named Dutch barn, Straw barn, Hay barn, Threshing barn and the Stone Dutch barn, which was home to a pair of lovely Barn owls, who nested there, every year.

All these buildings surrounded two large farmyards, each with its own double water trough. Every byre had a 'fodder-gang' like an extra stall, where hay was put down through a trap door in the floor of the hay barn above. What could be easier? No I don't think easy is the word I should use, as nothing was 'easy' on our farm in those days, one of the main reasons being, that we had neither gas nor electricity available to us, so every task had to be accomplished in the old style - mainly by guts and willpower.

Because of this, we had at least a dozen storm lanterns, better known as stable lamps. During dusk, or darkness, which ever building we entered, a lamp had to be carried in with us, and hung on any available crook, or low beam, until the task in hand was finished, then move the lamp with us, into the next building, as required. It became second nature to have a lamp hanging on our arm, even when we went to bed at night, a stable lamp went with us, and stood just within the door, providing not only a light, but a mild form of central heating too, and we were very glad of its friendly flame.

As I grew older, and left school, one of my jobs, was to keep all the lamps filled with paraffin oil, and to make sure the wicks were all trimmed straight, thus providing an 'even' glow. The lamp glasses had to be kept clean, allowing the light to shine through, and it was a "work of art" getting some of the glasses out of the wire frame, which surrounded the lamp. When this 'battle' was won, a handful of hay rubbed round inside the glass, kept it reasonably clean enough to use, but all glasses had to be thoroughly washed in hot water, once weekly, or more often if required, according to the time of year. We had great respect for all our stable lamps, as they played such a big part in our lives. Now a days, most houses have light, heat, and power, at a flick of a switch, but many is the time my mind wanders back to the time I couldn't have a reasonable light, until I'd trimmed the wick!

As children, we'd always helped around the farm, doing odd jobs both inside and outside the house. However, things altered drastically the day

I left school at fourteen years of age, on the 25th of July 1941, because on this same day - my Mother died, leaving my eldest sister Kitty, at nineteen years of age, to suddenly become housekeeper and “Mother’ as I had a younger sister still at school.

Another elder sister, Josie, helped at home for a while then had to go away, to work in a munitions factory to help the war effort, which left Kitty and I to do all that was necessary on such a large farm.

However, we just ‘got on with it’ as people did, in those days, and now, at seventy-four years of age, I’ve lived to tell the tale of how of how we did it!

The Farmhouse

We will first take a look at the farmhouse, which is the main building on any farm. Needless to say, it was a very big house, with five large bedrooms up the front stairs, plus the lad's communal bedroom, reached by a stone staircase, at the other end of the house. This very large room held seven beds, with room to spare. The front stairs were in two flights, with a long landing window half-way up. On this landing stood a glass case, filled with stuffed birds and a fox. Above the bedrooms were two large attics, where we stored our apples. Lying on the wooden floor, they kept good and sound until the following Spring.

A wide hall led to the front door, which opened directly onto the farmyard, we also had two parlours which we seldom had time to use. One was furnished, and Dad used it mainly as an office, where his desk was 'built in' under cupboards which had doors of beautiful natural walnut wood, as were both the parlour doors. I remember in the biggest parlour, the mat-frames were permanently set up, as there was always a half-made rag mat, waiting for us to have a few spare minutes to prod a few bits in.

Our big pantry, which was below ground level, had slate sconces all around it, with shelves above, and in the far corner was a wooden box about a yard square, with an open-mesh door. This was called the 'Safe' and was the nearest thing to a fridge, we had. The fair-sized back kitchen was stoned floored, and had a brown clay slopstone (a shallow sink). Into this, ran the only tap we had in the house, cold water of course, as we had no means of heating it, except by kettle or pan, on the coal fire.

Next we come to main room in the house, - the kitchen, which had to be seen to be believed, and is well worth describing. It was the largest farm kitchen in West Cumberland, and I have many times ridden round it on a pony or a bicycle. The stone flagged floor was scrubbed once per week, then wiped over with a cloth dipped in milk. This made the floor take on a shine, which helped to keep it clean. All the flags were bordered with white 'curly kews' put on with rubbing stone. It looked very nice when finished, but took one person (usually me) nearly half a day to wash.

Two very big kitchen windows looked out onto the farmyard, and both had dark brown painted shutters, so we had no need for curtains. The

St. Helens Farmhouse

ceiling comprised of large wooden beams, with lime-washed plaster between, and at one end, was suspended a huge wooden pulley, used for drying clothes. Large hooks were screwed into the beams at the other end of the ceiling, these being used to hang hams, and sides of bacon. Along one full side of the kitchen wall, stood the old farmhouse dresser, reaching from floor to ceiling, and on one end of it stood a large brown stone jar with an ornamental lid. This held the cure for all ills, - goose grease. If anyone had a sore throat, or a bad chest, they were rubbed back and front with it, and it wasn't long until they were fit for work again, otherwise they got a double dose!

A full set of Toby Jugs in various sizes decorated the top shelf of the dresser; other shelves holding dinner plates, soup dishes and such like, with all the cups and mugs hanging on hooks. The very bottom shelf held all the 'Adam and Eve' china, only used at christenings, weddings and funerals. On the short wall, beside the wooden 'settle' stood the Grandfather clock, respected by everyone, because whatever else went wrong, the clock was always right, it's chimes echoing through the house, so there was no excuse for being late, or meals not ready for the lads coming in. On the wall either side of the Grandfather clock, hung two large pictures, with wide gilt ornate frames. One was 'The Laughing Cavalier', and the other one -'When Did You Last See Your Father?' On the other short wall, stood our old walnut piano, which always looked out of place, but couldn't be done without.

Two tables stood in the kitchen, a short one in the corner beside the oven, and above this, were three large cupboards, where all the veterinary books were kept, plus a great variety of animal medicines, and a horrible looking weapon called a castrator. I never saw it actually being used, but knew exactly what it could achieve! The big long table, permanently covered with table-oilcloth, was where we all sat for meals. It covered the full length of the long wall, and was surrounded by forms and stools, with the 'carver's' chair at the top. Above this long table hung the biggest lamp, a brass contraption, which had a tall glass chimney, and was filled with paraffin every day. It hung on chains, which worked like a pulley, being pulled down to light, then pushed back up again, out of the way, while we ate our meal. Later on, we got an Aladdin lamp, still on a pulley, still needing oil, but it boasted a mantle which, when lit, shed a much brighter light. The other half of the kitchen was lit by two stable lamps, though we once had a Tilley lamp here, but it had to be pumped, before lighting, and Dad reckoned it was too 'fiddly'.

Like in any other farm kitchen, the main feature was the fireplace, which measured approx. ten feet across, seven feet high, and was polished to perfection with old-fashioned zebo blacklead. To the left of the fire, was a big boiler with a brass tap, never used for boiling water, but was kept full of dry kindling sticks. These were always warm, therefore easy to light a fire with, early morning, or to boost a flame under the kettle or a pan, when necessary. On the other side of the fire, was a large oven, with a polished steel door, with three brass damper knobs above it, used to 'draw' the flames towards the oven.

The actual fire itself, was two feet wide, with a 'jockey bar' stuck out at the front. This was made of thick steel, and had 'Home Sweet Home' cut out, in capital letters, with a design of wild flowers all around it. Below this, was the 'tidy', which hid the 'well' where all the ashes dropped into, and it had to be emptied every morning. The tidy was black, and brass bound, and in front of it was the fender made of polished steel, which was rubbed with emery paper twice weekly, to keep it shining. The fender was six feet long and slotted between it, lay the poker, tongs, and colerake, plus a small fire shovel kept there for handiness.

Above the fire, swung a big black hook, on a chain, which was where we hung the porridge and potato pans etc. to boil. This chain was fastened to a loose swivelled bar, which could be swung out, away from the fire, so we could stir the contents of the pan without getting burnt. This bar was called a bewl, and a very useful thing it was, too.

Over and above all this, was the mantle-piece, which was a showpiece in it's own right. The tea caddy stood in the middle, - this being a large black enamel tin, decorated with bunches of red roses, which surrounded a picture of Queen Victoria. A couple of genuine horseshoes stood either side of it, plus a few pairs of different sized brass candlesticks. Somewhere among all these stood a "Black Sambo" moneybox, made of metal. When a coin was put in his hand, he lifted it up and popped it into his month. A large velvet pincushion hung at one end of the mantle piece and a Rechabites Almanac at the other. We mustn't forget the fender stool, six inches high, specially made to fit the length of the fender, and covered with table oilcloth, which was easy to wipe, as the cats liked to sit here, when they managed to get sneaked into the house. I think they liked to rub themselves on the prodded hearthrug, which lay in front of the fender stool, but they were very soon jumped out of the way, when the kettle on the hob spit out, as it started to boil.

To complete the picture of the farmhouse fireplace, mention must be made of the cockroach trap, which lay permanently between the tidy and the fender. It was the size of a large dinner plate, made of tin, and looked like a fruit bowl with a hole in the bottom, but turned upside down. The sides were concaved, and roughened like sandpaper, which made it easy for the cockroaches to climb up. Four steel wires were suspended across the hole at the top, with a very small pie tin in the centre where the wire crossed, and into this was put a spoonful of jam, or beer. Each wire had two 'fly wings' so when the cockroach stood on the wire, to reach the jam, the 'fly wings' capsized, and the insect dropped into the hollow tin, and couldn't escape. Very ingenious it was, and very successful, too.

We kept a roaring fire going continuously, and could put two big logs on it, then throw a bucket full of coal on top, and it would hardly be noticed. We had no option but to keep a good fire burning, even in mid-summer, because everything at all we ate, had to be cooked on the fire, or in the oven beside it. Kitty baked six large loaves daily, besides all the 'biskies' and scones, plus big slabs of 'Sally cake' to cut up for the lads teas, which they carried out with them, to wherever they happened to be working. There was a permanent smell in the kitchen, of fresh baking which was almost as time- taking as washing day.

This was every Monday, as regular as clockwork, so by six o'clock in the morning, we had the fire burning in the grate under the big set-pot (boiler) outside in the wash-house, so we could have a supply of hot water, first lot of water boiled, was used to scald the calf and pig meal. Only after this was done, could we begin washing day. We had three large wooden tubs (casks) with iron bands round them, each having it's own 'poss stick' and rubbing board. Apart from these, we had a scrubbing brush each, plus red carbolic soap, a dolly-blue bag, paddy soap powder, robin starch, and a never-ending supply of elbow grease.

Our mangle was like something left behind by Methusella, made in cast iron, with a contraption on top, which we could screw down, to make the rollers nip tighter together, so squeeze more water out of the clothes. These rollers were solid wood, and heaven help anyone who got their fingers caught between them, especially if someone else was turning the handle! Butter cloths, and anything connected with the dairy, had all to be washed, boiled, and starched first, then followed our clothes, and the bedding, and towels etc. We finished with a never- ending supply of khaki shirts, and long woollen stockings, then the corduroy britches went through last.

As we got things washed and rinsed, we put them through the mangle twice, then hung them outside (weather permitting) on a wire clothesline, to dry. The washing had all to be done and out of the way, by two o'clock, because by that time, the water had to be boiled again, ready to scald the calf-meal for their evening feed.

As the washing dried, we ironed it, and this was a work of art, because we had an ancient box-iron, which used heaters, and was very temperamental. Heaters were one-inch thick pieces of iron, shaped like a shield, measuring five inches by three. These were dropped into the fire, where they stayed until red hot, then a long pair of tongs were used, to insert the heater, by the means of a trap door, at the mouth end of the iron. From then on, it was 'all go' to get as many clothes ironed as possible before the heater went cold. When this happened, it had to be returned to the fire for reheating, so we always had two heaters on the go, - one in the iron, and one in the fire. We also had two flat irons warm on the hob, for use between heaters getting warmed. Despite all this hassle, we managed to have all the washing done, dried, ironed, and up on the pulley to air, by late Monday night, so we could have a clear day on Tuesday, for the churning. So our weeks went by - every day bringing it's own work, and every season it's different needs, but somehow or other, we got it all done, and thought nothing of it!

The Hired Lads

On a mixed farm such as we had, life was run to routine, according to whether it was Spring, Summer, Autumn or Winter. Every season brought it's own work, yet there was always something to look forward to. One of the main things we enjoyed, was the holiday week, which happened twice annually, at Whitsuntide, and Martinmas. There were officially called 'Term Weeks' but were known in the farming community as 'Teerum'. All the hired lads took holiday then, and the family had to manage as best we could, usually helped by neighbours, and we only did what was really essential.

Besides being holiday week, two particular things took place at this time, - it was the local 'fair' week, also hiring time. The fair provided all sorts of amusements, - rolling pennies, slot machines, merry-go-rounds, swing boats, dodgem cars, ghost trains, coconut shies, plus many other attractions, mostly owned by the Taylor Bros., who knew exactly when to stage the fairs in a particular locality, because the farm workers only got paid once every six months, and this was at Term Week, therefore they usually had a bit of spare cash in their pockets at fair time.

Many a tale has been told about farm lads meeting a new sweetheart on these occasions, and taking her straight into the near-by fortune-tellers caravan, to hear what was forecast, regarding the situation. After listening to the gypsy's words of wisdom, it has been known for the lad to drop a lass there and then, without so much as a backward glance. Cumbrian lads didn't take chances! Any lad who already had a steady girlfriend, always spent a few coppers, and bought her a small trinket. This was known as a fairing, and to receive one of these from a lad, was almost as good as a promise to marry.

Yes, I do believe these fairings were the forerunners to an engagement ring, as many of the lads just went to the fair to be on the look-out for a likely lass, who gave the impression she would make a hard-working farmer's wife. Often enough, he wasn't only seeking a prospective wife, but employment too, because Term Week was the time to leave one job, and start another, if they desired. Each lad was hired for six months at a time, and when that period ended, if the farmer was satisfied with his work, he would ask the lad to continue being employed by him during the next six months ahead. This was known as 'stopping on', but if he

Hired Lads

thought the lad wasn't making much effort, he could pay him his dues, then dismiss him, and the lad would have to seek other employment.

This worked both ways, because if the lad wasn't satisfied with his employer, he could tell the farmer he was leaving, collect the wages due to him, then pack his belongings. So during the week before the term end, Dad had to ask each of his lads the same question - "Ista stoppun on?" If some of them decided to leave, it was then up to Dad to find a replacement. This was another reason for the fair "doing the rounds" at this particular time of year, because it was here the 'hirings' took place, meaning that any lad or lass looking for farmwork, - this is where they went, - to the hiring fair. These were held mainly at Cockermouth on the local auction mart, as the farmers were already there.

Once at the fair, - any lad looking for work, would 'hang about' and make it plain why he was there. Some would stand with a piece of straw between his lips, - a sure sign that he was available for hire, then immediately he got a job, the straw would be discarded. Often, there were more lads than farmers, so it paid them to be clean and tidy on the day, and not look "feckless". I well remember Dad once coming home, telling us he had hired a lad who was "short tongued, luckt a bit leet, nut ower clean, but had a good straang back und would luck better after a good feed ur two!"He was right, and the lad proved to be a decent honest worker.

To get back to the hiring fair, - after the farmer had a good look round the lads; he usually asked a few of them which part of the County they wanted to work in. Then after he had singled one out, and satisfied himself that the lad was sound in wind and limb, he would try and strike a bargain with him, and maybe get him hired for the next six months. Again, if the lad didn't like the look of the farmer, he was quite at liberty to say 'no'. This often happened if the lad had heard that this particular farmer didn't feed his lads too well. This was known locally as a farmer who 'kept a bad meat shop', and once word got around to this effect, the chap in question often had great difficulty persuading lads to hire with him. However, if they took to each other, and struck a deal, then the bargain was sealed, with a shake of hands, and often enough a florin, or half a crown was given to the lad, as a sign of good faith that he would turn up at the farm on Sunday morning ready to begin work.

More often than not, the lad would call the previous day, to borrow a horse and cart, to transport his 'box' or trunk from his home, to his new abode. This one trunk contained all the lad possessed, and it was trundled around with him, from one farm to another, wherever he happened to be

Our first tractor

hired at. It stood at his bedside, which was nearly always in a room shared with all the other hired lads. This bedroom at St Helen's Farm held seven lads without any difficulty, with room for more, if needed.

The first thing the "Missis" did, when a new lad arrived was show him his own bed, and he kept that particular bed, all the time he was hired with us. Next thing to be done, was to show him his place at the table, and (like the bed) he kept that one spot until he was told different, because in those days, where you sat at the table, showed exactly what position you held on the farm. Dad sat at the top of the table, in the carver's chair, because he was the boss. Next to him sat the cowman, then the horseman. Next came the shepherd, then the longest serving hired lad, followed by the others. At the front of the table the 'Misses' (my sister) sat, next to the boss, then came any daughters of the family, with the servant lass at the bottom, if there was one. So when a hired lad first arrived, he too, sat at the bottom of the table, and it was a red-letter day for him, if one of the other lads left, and he moved up one seat higher in the pecking order. All this sounds a very old fashioned method now, but it always worked, everyone knew their own place, so there was never any arguments, and strike was a word never heard.

As time went by, these hired lads very soon got into the way of things, and felt quite at home, often forgetting to write home and let their parents know that all was well. (Note that hired lads were always referred to, as 'lads' even though some were well past middle age). Usually, when any of them married, they found other lodgings, and left the communal bedroom behind. As time progressed, in approx. 1942 onwards, most hired lads got paid by the week. We never had less than eight lads working for us, at St Helens, plus the family. No farm requires a great number of staff now, due to mechanisation, and life is not such hard graft. Hiring fairs are no longer held, - there being no need for them.

Thinking of all the different lads who worked with us over the years, - four individuals stick out in my mind. Ike was the elderly one, who let me have his treasured 'sweet ration' coupons, which were allocated during the war. In exchange for these, I kept his best leather boots clean and polished. Young Jim was the lively one, always full of fun, who eventually became a policeman on the docks. Another lad's name was Joseph William, but known to all on the farm as 'Cocker' and it didn't matter which part of the farm he was working in, - his Mother always turned up with a basin full of hot chips, at twelve o'clock, for his dinner, having walked through Aigle Ghyll woods to reach him! Needless to say he lodged at home with his Mother, and she idolised him, - much to the other lad's amusement.

Last but not least, was Ben, who was from Moor Row. Ben's wages would be about four pounds weekly at this time, and every Saturday morning without fail, he got a 'letter' from home. Inside the envelope, was just another envelope ready stamped and addressed to his Mother. Ben had to put a pound note in this envelope, and have it in the post before Monday, and this he did regularly. Only once I remember him forgetting, and on the Tuesday afternoon, his Mother arrived by bus, demanding to know "what was going on?" We didn't get a visit from the postman every day, but we could guarantee he would call every Saturday!

Ben once got drunk, but managed to cycle up the lane, and into the farmyard, then he cycled twenty-five times round the cobble-stoned enclosure, because he couldn't find the way out! Actually, young Jim had closed both gates as a joke, then stood and watched, until the poor frustrated cyclist fell off! Ben eventually went into the army, and joined the "Glorious Gloucesters " and I remember Dad saying "God help them!"

Funnily enough when the war ended, in 1945, we held a grand 'Victory Party' in our big farmhouse kitchen, and Ben actually turned up, to join in the celebrations. After the party, we all went to 'Long and Small' at Flimby, where a huge bonfire was lit, on the shore, and we all danced round it, while I played the piano accordion. Ben was hailed as a hero, along with another local soldier who happened to be on leave, and both were feted accordingly. I remember Ben staggering into the farmhouse safely, around midnight, but I don't think he managed the stairs!

Horses

Enough has been said about the human side of life on the farm, - now let us move to the animals. Animals! - the very word conjures up anything from a mouse to an elephant, but when we particularly mention farm animals, - that is another matter. I want to describe now, the biggest animals we had, on our farm - the horses. Not just every-day horses, but the Clydesdales, - that grand breed of horses which seemed to have 'England' stamped all over them, - strong, sturdy, honest, and dependable. Only a good understanding horseman could take a young Clydesdale, and break it in, fit for work. I've watched our horseman, Bob Courty, spend many a long day, trailing around behind a young horse, with nothing but a bridle and driving reins on it, with a big heavy plank of wood dragging behind, to let the animal get the feel of a bit of weight.

As the days went by, this plank was made heavier, by adding chains to it. After a while, the horse had a collar put on, then the hames. Later, the saddle and breechings were added, until it got used to wearing gear, and hearing the rattle of chains behind it. Eventually, when Bob thought it was time to yoke the young horse into a block cart, for the first time, two

'Daisy' decorated with carnival gear.
Photo courtesy of 'Times and Star'.

lads held it's head, one at either side, while he put the harness on, and fastened the belly-band. Finally, it was fully ycked, and away it went, twice round the yard, led by the two lads holding it's head, then out onto the lane with just Bob driving it.

A sight worth seeing, was a young Clydesdale taking it's first steps out into the world as a working horse, though it still had a lot to learn. For instance, it had to be taught to stand quiet in it's own stall. Not only that, it had to learn how to lie down, when in the stable, because if any farmer bought a horse in an auction, or in a sale, then discovered it wouldn't lie down when indoors, this was considered to be a major fault, then the farmer could return the animal, and demand his money back. Such were the rules and regulations in the farming community.

However, once the horse got broken in to work, there was always plenty waiting for it, - pulling the plough, harrows, discs, digger, turnip drill, binder etc, to mention but a few, - horsepower was always in demand. The horses were very well catered for, because the farmer knew he couldn't survive without them, so made sure they always had plenty of good warm bedding, plus a plentiful supply of crushed oats and hay to eat, when the elements were against them feeding outside. On the arrival of Spring, it was a joy to see them turned out to grass, when all the horses young or old, would roll on their backs, kicking their legs into the air, obviously feeling it was good to be alive.

Besides having it's own stall, - each horse had it's own name, such as Jewel, Lofty, Prince Tommy, Darling, among others. We just had one lighter type of horse, - a Vanner, called Teddy, who was used to pull the Spring cart, or the trap, both these being used as 'people carriers'. Teddy was more pony-like, and could trot for long distances, so because of this, he was used for travelling into Flimby, our nearest village, to collect groceries, or to the Railway Station if needed. Teddy was a handy horse to have around, but it was the Clydesdales who carried the weight of work, starting the season with ploughing.

Such was the amount of ploughing needed, we very often had two drafts of horses, each pulling a double furrowed plough, and a single horse with smaller plough standing by, to go round the headriggs etc. Dad reckoned that a good ploughman was worth a fortune, but a good even-matched pair of horses was worth two! Wise words, I would say, - no doubt spoken from experience. I have known two ploughmen work all through the night, by the light of the moon, if the ground was in good fettle, as Cumberland has always been noted for changeable weather, which could hold up the proceedings without a moments notice, therefore it was advisable to carry on while the going was good, using 'fresh' horses of course. Nothing looks nicer than a newly ploughed field, when the furrows are straight, before the discs and harrows play their part, breaking up the soil, preparing it for stitching, or sowing corn, as the case may be. Being on the coast, the ploughs were always followed by the inevitable flock of seagulls, swooping over the upturned earth, in search of grub, but I can't remember the birds 'working' night shift, when the ploughman did!

However, the horses weren't always pulling implements, - sometimes they had a block cart behind them. These were cumbersome, awkward looking carts, usually made from solid oak, with straight heavy shafts, and two big wooden - spoked wheels, bound in iron. Later on, wheels were made smaller, with rubber tyres, which no doubt made the cart easier for the horse to pull, but to me, they never 'blended' with the block cart, and always looked out of place.

Just outside the farmyard, through two large green double-doors, was the purpose- built midden, where all the dung from the calf-pens and cow byres, was dumped every day. This was spread on the fields, mainly in Springtime, or when needed. After this job was finished, all the block-carts got well scrubbed down, and given a fresh coat of paint, always in bright colours, - blue, orange, red, and yellow, but I cannot recall the Spring cart being any other colour than dark green.

Yes, a Clydesdale horse had a hard life, but not without it's lighter moments. Every Sunday morning, weather permitting, all the lads mounted a horse each, and rode them bareback down the farm lane, over the main road, then across the railway lines, and down onto the shores of the Solway Firth. Then across the sands, and straight into the tide, to freshen the horses, and wash the mud from their legs. There were usually eight horses, and most of them enjoyed the event, cantering up and down the waves for quite a while. However, our big white horse, old Fred, was the exception to the rule, and didn't appreciate his weekly bath. So after being in the water for just a few minutes, he would lie down, roll over, then get up immediately, and was back on dry land, before his rider realised what was happening, and the poor lad had a wet weary walk back

Mabel and Malcolm

to the homestead, to find old Fred back in the stable looking quite unconcerned. Needless to say, it was always one of the younger lads who drew the short straw with Fred, - the older ones having encountered the experience many times before!

Another vivid memory I have, is the blacksmith coming to our farm at regular intervals, to shoe the horses. His name was Tom Frith, living in Workington. He was the official blacksmith for the St Helen's Colliery at Siddick, and as our farm belonged to the colliery, he kept our horses well shod too. Tom was a big man, with rosy cheeks, iron-grey hair, and wore a long leather apron, which reached floor level. He always arrived in time for breakfast, which was half past seven, and joined the lads at the big table. Every morning, except Sundays, we made oatmeal porridge to start off the breakfast, and Tom never failed to dig his spoon into the centre of his basin, to test the contents, and if the spoon didn't stay upright, he declared the porridge to be "ower wattery" and not fit to eat! This verdict was never a surprise, and didn't bother us at all as we had plenty of good fresh bread and butter to satisfy his healthy appetite.

After breakfast, he would wend his way to the smithy, situated two hundred yards away from the farmhouse. Again, this was a relic left behind by the old original colliery, left intact specifically for the farm's benefit. As a child, it gave me great pleasure to run down to the smithy, and watch old Tom light his fire with 'small' coal brought especially for the job. He made it burn brighter by using the very large bellows behind it, which were pumped by hand. When the fire was really glowing, he would heat a large length of iron until it was red hot, then using his tongs, carry it to the anvil. Here he would hammer it, turn it, and twist it, until within a few moments, it started to take shape, then suddenly, it would be a perfect horseshoe.

I never ceased to marvel at the way he did it, with such accuracy. When satisfied with the shape, he would drop it into an old barrel, filled with cold water. How it hissed! Steam soon hit the roof, and escaped through the slack slates. While the shoe was cooling, he took the horse's foot between his knees, to remove any old nails from the hoof, then fasten on the new shoe, using a short shafted hammer and long nails with a square head. Finally, he rubbed the whole hoof over, with a long file, making sure there were no snaggy bits round the new shoe.

Sometimes, one of the horses (usually Mabel) had a lighter shoe fitted, - this happened when the horse was needed for the annual village carnival, to draw one of the decorated lorries, perhaps holding a queen and her retinue round the streets of the village. When this happened, not only were the horse's feet given first class treatment, but everything about it was, too. It's coat got well brushed, then mane and tail plaited, before being tied with ribbon, but the main attraction was the harness, which was black leather, polished to perfection, then decorated with brass. Three sets of brass bells adorned the collar, hames and saddle, with at least a dozen different brasses on the martingeld. All the buckles were brass, too, besides fancy studs on the breechings and backband. All this brass, was the horseman's pride and joy, and it only saw daylight on carnival day, which was a highlight in our farming calendar. Since about 1970, decorated horses have disappeared from local carnivals, - tractors and trailers having taken their place.

It is the same with farming too, every farm has at least one tractor, some having two or three. We bought our first tractor, a Fordson Major, approx. 1944, which we found greatly beneficial, but still kept the horses for much of the work. The lads nicknamed the tractor "The iron horse" but old Ike, who had been a horseman for many years, always referred to it as "that tin thing" and never really accepted it as an asset. Though tractors are almost indispensable in our area now, I am glad to see the Clydesdales still appear at local showgrounds. Long may they flourish.

I never did profess to being a scholar, especially where history is concerned, but whenever I hear that tale about the English king, who once stood up and shouted "my kingdom for a horse!" - I'm inclined to think it wouldn't have been such a bad swap after all!

Pit Ponies

Because our farm belonged to St Helen's Colliery, we were under contract to provide food for the pit ponies, which lived and worked permanently underground, down the mine at Siddick, where they hauled bogies filled with coal from the coal-face to the shaft, before it was brought up to ground level. One of the men, who looked after the ponies underground, was called Benny Moore, who lived in a cottage not far from our farm, so I knew him well, and felt I knew the ponies too, because he often talked about them, saying how hard they worked, sometimes in appalling conditions. Despite this, they were very well cared for, and got every attention. According to Benny they were his 'family' and he saw to their every need.

In one of our barns, set apart from the rest, there was a special machine called a hay-chopper. My Uncle Willie worked full time in this barn, preparing the fodder for the pit ponies. Straw and chaff were used as 'bedding' with crushed corn and chopped hay for eating, plus the odd sack of carrots. Though our own horses ate hay straight from the loft, hay for the pit ponies had to be chopped fine. This was taken to the colliery by horse and cart, as long as I could remember, before then, it had been transported via the little 'donkey engine' which run on the railtrack along the shore.

One very memorable occasion happened when I was a teenager, because the colliers called a strike, and as it was likely to be prolonged, the powers that be, decided that the pit ponies should be brought to the surface, and taken for a 'holiday' to our farm. Before they could be brought up the shaft, each pony's head was put in a hessian sack, which was tied round the neck. This was to avoid the ponies getting a shock, as their eyes were not accustomed to daylight.

When they arrived at the farm, they were put in the Croft, - the field nearest the homestead, so we could keep an eye on them, making sure they didn't start kicking, and harming each other. Benny, and another man stayed, and 'talked' to them for a couple of days, until they settled. Only then were the sacks removed, and soon they were eating fresh grass, which was a complete change of diet for them. They numbered about a dozen, and stayed with us a month. Needless to say, - they became quite friendly, and I know I wept when they were taken back to Siddick, put down the pit, and made to resume work, but such is life, and I couldn't do anything about it.

Before we leave this chapter, I want to record here, the humorous true story of an event which took place, concerning a horse called Spider, who came as a 'lodger' to our farm, while it's owner went abroad for a few months. It was a leggy, racey - type horse, definitely not a 'working model'. Because of this, the lads thought they would enter it to race at Workington Agriculture Show, but Dad explained to them, that it would have to be taught to run round a course, and not in a straight line. This didn't appear to worry them, and they practised Spider every night, racing round our Stackyard, timing him with an old tin alarm clock.

Our smallest lad, was called Lennie, so it was decided that he would be the jockey, wearing his usual cord britches, kytle jacket, black leather clogs with brass nebs, and his cap turned back to front. Then came a real stroke of luck, - the Show Secretary asked Dad if they could use one of our big fields for the race, as the show field was a bit overcrowded. This, of course, delighted the lads, so they took 'our' horse to the field every spare night they had, and raced it round the course, - through the gate, past the sheep troughs, round the old oak tree, then straight down the

Siddick Colliery where the pit ponies worked.
Photo courtesy of 'Times and Star'.

middle of the field to the winning post, - how could they fail? The show day dawned fine and sunny, so Dad gave the lads an hour off work, to attend the race, knowing they would go, anyway, because they had each put a small bet on.

When all the horses lined up for the race, Spider looked quite at home, because after all, - he was at home, with Lennie dressed in his every-day 'silks' complete with brass nebbed clogs. Bang! The horses got off to a start, and away galloped Spider, past the troughs, round the old oak tree, at a terrific speed. Lennie glanced over his shoulder, - not another horse in sight, - he was winning! It was only when he turned onto the straight run in, that disaster struck, - all the other horses were galloping towards him! It was only then that Lennie realised he was going the wrong way round the course! Even if Lennie had known this, before the race, nothing in this world would have persuaded Spider to go in any other direction than the one he'd been trained to follow without fail, every night the past six weeks. What did Lennie do? Just kept on galloping past the winning post, straight through the open gate, across two more fields, then home.

Of course the lads lost their money, but the race kept them laughing for a week. They definitely learnt something that day, - nothing is a certainty in this world, - especially when involves horse racing!

Cows

Ask any small child what sort of animals live on a farm, and ninety percent will say "cows". Plenty of these we had on our farm, mainly milk cows, but a fair share of fatstock too. In 1939, our milk herd was half Ayrshire and half Shorthorn, but as time went on, we slowly turned to the Friesians, and by the late 1940's these were very popular. We had three main milking byres, each with a fodder-gang at one end, and a big window at the other end, which had iron bars across it, to prevent the glass being broken, as cows rubbed themselves against it.

A low, broad whitewashed beam ran full length of each byre, and turned upside down on this, were the milking coppies, - small wooden three-legged stools, which the lads used to sit on, while milking the cows. All the byre walls, ceilings, and stalls, were white washed regularly. Each stall held two cows, each one having its own trough, also a drinking bowl, where cold, clean water was available at all times. The two cows had one salt lick between them, this being fastened to the wall, between the two troughs, where both cows could reach it. This salt lick, which was the size of a building brick, provided the cows with all the minerals they needed, whilst sleeping indoors during the winter months.

In every stall, standing upright between the two cows, was a long steel pole, which reached from floor to ceiling, and commonly called a 'Rud Stiaak" (Rood Stake). The bands, which circled each cows neck, were fastened loosely to this, and slid up and down, according to whether the animal was standing up or lying down. Actually, they were chains, but were never called anything else other than cow bands. The Sanitary Inspector called on a regular basis, to inspect the byres, and all the dairy utensils etc. His name was Mr Nelson, from Cockermouth, commonly named in farming fraternity as "Lord Nelson". A likeable chap, and always thorough, but wasted a lot of our time, when he visited, approx. once every two months and I always looked upon him, as being an intruder.

The cows were milked twice daily, at half past six early morning and five o'clock each evening. As no electricity was available, all milking was done by hand, sitting on a copy, with a clean scrubbed bucket between the knees, the side of the lad's face pressed tightly against the cow's belly. Ha! - I can picture them yet, - buckets full of warm, steaming, frothy milk, being carried across the farmyard, past the stables, behind the farmhouse, before it reached the 'cooling house'. Here the milk was poured into a big tin, similar to a small bath, with a tap on the front. This tin was set high on a shelf, and when the tap was opened, the milk trickled gently down the cooler. This was very similar, in shape and size, to a zinc rubbing board, as used in the washhouse, but was stood upright. It was hollow, and as the milk flowed over it, cold water from a "spring' was run through inside it, thus cooling the milk, as it ran into a ten-gallon milk tin, placed underneath. I doubt very much if this method would pass the Sanitary Inspector now, yet it always chilled the milk, and we never had any problems. Every drop of milk was siled twice, - as it entered the cooler, and again when it left. We used gauze bottoms in the siles, and 'clover leaf' cotton wool sile pads, which caught any small particles of dirt etc. which might have entered the milk, between leaving the cow and reaching the cooler.

After all this was done, the bulk of the milk, about twenty-five gallons, was stood aside. Ten gallons were put into a special tin, to await collection by Harry Cape, who lived in the Post Office at Siddick, and retailed milk around the village, using a small flat cart and a pony called

Bottling the milk

Polly. He later acquired a small grey van, which rattled dreadfully as he drove up the rough farm lane. Dad used to say it was a wonder the milk wasn't churned into butter, before it ever reached Siddick, but we never had any complaints.

Other milk was put into tins, each bearing a brass plate, with our own official number on. Every morning, these tins, containing approx. twenty-five gallons of milk, from two milkings, were lifted onto the 'Spring Cart', pulled by Teddy, and Dad took it to the Railway Station, at Flimby, almost two miles away, to board the 9.15am train to Aspatria, where it was delivered to the Milk Marketing Depot. Here it was checked, by the number on the brass plate, and we got a cheque in payment, monthly, from Thames Ditton, in Surrey.

Milk not sent to Aspatria was dealt with in an entirely different way. While still warm, it was put through a 'separator', - a large zinc bowl, with two moveable spouts and a tap. When milk left the tap, it hit a float, which directed it into the magic bit of the device This consisted of fourteen cone-shaped discs, in an iron casing, resting on a thick rubbed ring. Somehow or other, this fancy contraption separated the milk, - cream running out of one spout, into a bucket, and skimmed milk out of the other, into a ten-gallon tin. It was all worked by turning a big handle at the side. Again, I wonder what the Sanitary Inspector would say today, if he saw me cooling milk in one corner of the cooling house, with the separator working in another, and an oil lamp swinging on the beam between them, - I shudder to think.

That is beside the point, now to return to the separated milk, - the skimmed milk was fed to the calves, twice daily, sometimes with meal added, and the cream was kept to make butter. During winter, when the cows were lying in, they were fed with hay, crushed corn, and cow-cake, which was delivered to the farm in, slabs the size of a doormat. These were put through a cake-crusher, worked by hand of course, and came out in small pieces, which the cows managed to chew. We also had a turnip cutter, which cut the turnip into shreds, for the cows, so they were well catered for. On odd occasions, during the war, we managed to get a few bags of foodstuff called UVEKA, which looked very like large cornflakes, made of maize. Mixed among this, was a lot of large bean-like brown objects about four inches in length, called locusts, which were, sweet, very 'chewy' and good to eat. (I can verify this!)

Feeding the calves

While we were at St Helens, a man called Elijah Cooper, from Seaton, started using cattle-trucks, for transporting animals. Previous to this, we walked them, either to Cockermouth or Workington. I well remember the time Dad and I were walking four heifers to the auction mart at Workington, three miles away. At that particular time, there was a stallholder's market on Washington Street every Wednesday, selling goods of every description. We had to drive our cattle along this street, and to shorten a long story, - one of our heifers had an 'argument' with a stall holding pots, pans, and china tea sets. Looking back, how I wish I'd a tape recorder, to record the conversation which took place then, between one frustrated stall-holder, and one irate farmer. I didn't hear the outcome, as I had hurried on, trying desperately to persuade the remaining three heifers to walk through the doors of the auction mart, at the other end of the same street. I eventually managed this, but not before one of them almost found it's way through the door of "Henderson's Photography" - what a super photograph it would have made!

Still on the subject of cattle on the road, I have told the true tale many times, about two neighbouring farmers who met, while each was driving a dozen cows in opposite directions. Knowing each other well, they naturally stopped for a crack, while the cattle grazed on roadside verges. When it was time to move on, they simply halved the herd, and went their separate ways, quite unconcerned as to whether they had their own cows or not, - such was life in the 'slow lane' and I cannot imagine this happening today.

Though fortunately we never experienced "foot and mouth" at St Helens, we once had a cow stricken with a dreaded ailment called "Anthrax". It died in a "'loose box' at the bottom of the yard, and because this was a very contagious disease, the carcase had to be burnt under police supervision. A large, deep hole was dug, in the 'Blinndy' field, into which was poured a few bags of lime. Wooden sleepers were laid across the hole, and on these, was built a huge bonfire, with the carcase in the middle of it. Over this, was poured a few gallons of paraffin, then it was set alight. Many people from the surrounding area came to watch the bizarre spectacle, and as the bonfire burned away, all the ashes and remnants dropped into the hole, which was then filled in by the original earth, leaving only a mound, as a reminder of what had taken place.

Because we were still schoolchildren when this happened, my younger sister Rene, and I, felt it had been an exciting experience, and actually asked Dad if he could burn another cow, the following week? I'll leave his answer to my reader's imagination, as it is definitely unprintable!

Now to mention one of the main animals on the farm, - Barney the bull, who'se stall was at the bottom of the longest byre. He was a roan shorthorn, and not only did he 'serve' our own cows, but those from surrounding farms, too, and was always kept in the peak of condition. As time went on, we got a younger Friesan bull called Freddie, but we kept Barney too. The bulls ate a lot of crushed corn, and we had our own corn crusher in the meal-house, worked by a petrol engine, which also worked the small threshing machine which was a permanent fixture in the straw barn. Malcolm always handled the bulls, and they didn't take kindly to strangers. Malcolm had very poor eye-sight, and couldn't read, so he had an interesting hobby. He plaited binder twine string, into very long lengths, and sewed them into a circle, using a packing needle, and they made super mats for the scullery.

Butter Making

After the milk had gone through the separator, the skimmed milk was used to feed the calves, and the cream was set aside, in the dairy, until Tuesday, when all the week's cream was put together ready for churning, which started immediately after breakfast. We had a big churn, like a big old-fashioned dolly tub lying on its side. It had open-work shelves inside, to break up the cream, as it was turned round and round by a handle at the side. One of the lads often helped us with the churning, as it was heavy work. The inside of the churn, was first scalded, then rinsed in clean cold water, before the cream was poured in.

The churn had a huge cork, measuring a foot across, this being fastened into place before churning began. We had to keep listening constantly, as we could hear when the cream 'broke', as the liquid began to run, and the fat 'clagged' together. This usually took about thirty minutes, but if the cream got stuck on one of the selves, and wouldn't roll off, the churn just flew round and round, making no noise at all. This was known as the churn "going to sleep", and I've seen us spend half a hour, jerking it backwards and forwards, to get it moving again. As soon as churning was finished, we started with the butter.

First of all, - everything likely to come into contact with the butter, had to be well scrubbed with hot water and oatmeal, including our hands, to prevent sticking. The fat was then taken from the churn, and piled onto to the 'butter worker' which was a long white-wood contraption on legs, almost like a table with its back up. It measured 2ft by 5ft, having slots at either end, for drainage. The butter was then well washed, with gallons of icy cold pure 'spring water' which ran from a special tap. It had to be well squeezed at the same time, to get all the whey out of it, but soon as clear water ran from the butter, it was then pure fat, and ready for salt. This had to be squeezed through and through the butter too, using bare hands, to get an even mixture.

During the winter months, when the cows weren't getting any fresh grass, the butter was almost white, so we added a few drops of 'colouring' to give it a richer colour. When all the squeezing and mixing was finished, it was plain sailing. The butter was weighed into pounds and half pounds, using brass scales, and layed out in rough oval shapes. We next needed the 'butter hands, these being flat pieces of wood,

Milk churn and butter clappers

approx. 9 inch by 4 inch, with short handles, and were used to clap the butter into shape, then the end product was laid in rows, on cool green Buttermere slates, in the dairy. However, if someone was having a christening or a wedding, and wanted to make a show, we had a small fancy mould, into which we pressed the butter, and when turned out, a rose was shown on top, but this was only for special occasions. Normally, it was just criss-crossed on top, and wrapped in greaseproof paper, until the following day, Wednesday, which was market day at Workington.

Early after breakfast, the goods were packed into 'butter baskets', which were large, shallow, and made of wickerwork, where the butter could be laid flat, before it was covered with clean white damask cloths. The basket had a strong handle, as we had to walk half a mile, down the farm lane, to catch the bus into Workington, which cost us threepence each for a return ticket. On arrival we visited certain shops where we knew our regular customers were waiting, - including Criags, on Hagg Hill, Mr Dand the ironmonger, Mabel Tracey's haberdashery shop, Salisbury's Gent outfitters, and Miss Coates, the high class outfitters. Butter left, we took it to the 'covered market' where stalls were available for people from outlying areas, to sell their wares.

One lady had a sweet stall, where she broke up slabs of home-made toffee, with a 'toffee hammer' and she knew exactly how many pieces weighed a quarter. A one-armed man sold fruit and vegetables, and on the next stall, were remnants, and curtain material. The market was always "vibrant", lots of noise, with cheery greetings exchanged between customers and stall-holders alike. It was here, among these good-natured market traders, we sold our butter, this being the highlight of my week, because we got a bit of crack, plus many a laugh.

We experienced difficulty during the Second World War, when rationing was imposed. Our 'regular' customers we kept, as they registered their ration books with us, but we were not allowed to sell on the open market. Any 'surplus' butter had to be deposited with Mrs Johnstone, at her grocery shop on Washington Street, where she sold it to her registered customers. After leaving here, our outing was never complete without paying a very short visit to Benn's Confectioners, as they had a small 'tea-room' upstairs, where we sat and enjoyed a welcome cup of tea, and a delicious buttered scone, and I don't think I have ever tasted such scones since, - what a lovely way to end our market-day visit to Workington.

Sheep

We've read about the horses and cows, so are left mainly with sheep, and what awkward things to be left with! If there is anything more contrary than a sheep, I have yet to find it. We kept quite a few different breeds over the years, but stuck mainly to Herdwicks, Swaledales, and Border Leicesters. Most were kept on fields parallel to the shore, where grass grew plentiful, but no shrubs or trees, which made it much easier to count sheep at a distance. Once every week, Granda would walk round all the fields containing any type of animal, - this being called 'looking the stock'. Every animal was counted, looked over, and had to be on it's feet, before he left the fields. During warm, damp weather, the sheep were apt to be attacked by the bluebottle fly, which ate into the skin, and laid eggs. When this happened, the sheep was said to be 'wickt' being easily seen to be 'off colour'. This meant they needed extra care, and such animals were attended to, everyday, using medicine, and green tar ointment as a ''wickt'' sheep was indeed a source of trouble.

I well remember Granda meeting the parish Vicar, one day, as he was working among the sheep, and the Vicar said "Ha, my good man, I see you are tending your flock, as I tend mine''. "Aye" answered Granda - " but if ah thowt ah'd hafe as many 'wickt' uns in my flock, as ah know thoo hez in thine, - ah'd droon hafe of thum, widoot batten a eye-lid!" To this day, I don't think the Vicar had any idea what he was talking about, but he meant every word he'd said, as he did when any of the lads got a cough, he would say "Stop barkun lad, thoo'se wuss nur a yow (ewe) on turnips!"

There were three main things connected with keeping sheep, - dipping, clipping, and lambing time. By law, all sheep had to be dipped at least once yearly, with the local policeman in attendance, to make sure the job was carried out correctly. We had proper purpose- built dipping tubs, and pens, adjoining the farm buildings, - two big pens about fifteen yards long, and two troughs eight feet deep, approx. twelve yards long. These two troughs, which were below ground level, and stone -lined, were parallel to each other. One was filled with water (nine parts cold to one part hot) to which, disinfectant was added. The sheep were put in individually, at one end, and had to swim to the other end, before scraffling up stone steps, to get out.

Kitty feeding pet lamb, note the old pit lamp cabin in background

The other trough, which wasn't quite so deep, had no water in, but three of the lads stood in it, wearing wellington boots, with the oldest clothes they possessed, knowing their shirts and overalls would only be fit for the ash-bin, when the dipping was finished. These three lads each held a long pole, and as the sheep passed them, in the adjoining trough, they had to make sure that every one went under the water. Even their heads had to be dipped, and to make certain this happened, the lads used their long poles to push the sheep under, hence they were actually submerged three times before they reached the steps.

When they were back in the pens, they had to stay put, until they 'dripped', and all the water off them, drained back into the trough. Only then, were the pen gates opened, and the flock went back into the field, while an other lot was rounded up, for their annual dip, and the ritual started all over again. After all the sheep had gone through the trough, the farm dogs were put in, too - providing we could find them, because they somehow sensed what was about to take place, and slyly disappeared, - wise dogs!

We used the same pens at clipping time, - shearing the sheep, which again had to be done by hand, using special stools to lay the sheep on, these being like low tables with slatted tops, but many of the older lads preferred to lay the sheep on the ground, - the hand shears working non-stop. One of the lads was kept constantly busy, sharpening shears, so there was always a spare pair ready for use, when necessary. It was a work of art getting the fleece off in one piece, starting behind the neck, and finishing at the tail. We had to have plenty of Elastophlast handy, if one of the lads was learning to clip for the first time, - this was for the lads fingers, - not the sheep! It looked so easy when the regulars were clipping but I've seen both sweat and tears flowing from many of the younger lads brave enough to "have a go".

The fleeces were then wrapped into bundles, - one fleece per bundle, each being tied securely, with a length of wool torn from the fleece. The bundles were then stored in the wool-house, until a wagon came from Carlisle to collect them. If we had an extra good quality fleece, Dad would have a blanket woven from it, or a travelling rug to wrap round our knees whilst sitting in the Spring-cart. Sometimes, if a sheep with a good skin died, Dad would skin the whole sheep, and make a rug, by stretching the skin, and nailing it taunt onto the inside of a barn door. When it dried, he would wipe the skin over, with a paraffin rag, once weekly, then let it dry again. It took about eight weeks, and the finished article cost only threepence for the paraffin, and after washing, they were beautiful.

Lambing time was springtime, keeping us busy until late at night, with all the expectant ewes being put in the croft, - a large field adjoining the homestead, where they were handy to keep an eye on. Just over a hundred lambs was our average yield, if we had a good season, but things often went wrong, and we were left with a pet lamb or two, to torment us. Some people, who aren't farmers, think cuddly pet lambs are a gift from heaven, but we looked upon them as a gift from the devil himself, because they were a downright nuisance, - innocent though they were.

If a ewe had died during the birth, or had abandoned her lamb for any reason, Dad would bring the poor little waif into the house, wrapped in a hessian bag, and lie it on the fender in front of the fire, and it was up to us lasses to make sure it rallied. We had to learn it to take milk, by putting two fingers down it's throat, encouraging it to suck with it's tongue. This didn't take long, if the lamb had any strength at all, and we soon had it taking milk from a bottle with a rubber teat on. Before many days passed, we seemed to spend half our time putting milk into them at one end, and wiping up after them at the other, but once we got them "on the bottle" - out they went, into a spare dry calf pen, with plenty of straw, and could they blare! They were better than an alarm clock any day, and had to be attended to, at regular intervals.

If we had a good ewe lose it's lamb, Dad would take the skin from it's new born dead lamb, and wrap it round the body of one of the pet lambs, then try to persuade the ewe to 'mother' it. This ruse didn't work very often, but well worth a try. When the lambs were a fortnight old, they were brought into the farm yard to have their tails 'docked' (cut short) Granda usually did this, using a razor sharp knife, thus helping keep their hinnder ends clean, often preventing them from getting wickt.

When a lamb had been hand-reared, it was always difficult getting it to blend in with the flock. Somehow or other, it stuck out like a sore thumb, and Dad wasn't keen on this, as it unsettled the other sheep. I remember him once sending me to the auction mart at Workington, with such a lamb, a few months old. I put it in the Spring-cart, covered with a heavy net, to keep it in, and off I went. Eventually, I got my horse right up to the auction door, then went to seek assistance. Out came this young lad, who obviously hadn't ever had dealings with a pet lamb before, and despite my warning, he just threw back the net, out leapt the lamb, and away like a rocket, - fortunately in the right direction. The lad stood dumbfounded, before asking me what I was going to do about it. I answered "I delivered it lad, - you catch it!" then left him to enjoy the experience.

I remember another special pet lamb we had, during wartime, when Dad was allocated petrol for his car, to be used for 'business purposes' only. At that particular time, my brother Cyril, was keen on a girl who lived at Lamplugh, so he attended the local dances held in that area, travelling by bicycle. However, one very stormy night, he had the brainy idea of borrowing Dad's car, instead of getting wet. In order to make it 'legal' he put our pet lamb on the back seat of the little Austin 7, hoping to convince any policeman who may have stopped him, that he was taking it to a prospective buyer. (At midnight?)

Full of confidence, he set off, and in due course, - parked the car outside the hall, where he enjoyed the dance, especially when the girl in question accepted his offer of a lift home. Due to the blackout, she never noticed the 'passenger' on the back seat, and had just settled down in the front, when the lamb blared loudly, frightening the poor lass out of her wits. Before Cyril could offer any sort of explanation, she leapt from the car, and vanished into the darkness, taking with her any chance of a budding romance.

However, the lamb must have enjoyed the trip out, because the following day, when Dad opened the car door, it jumped in before him, and made itself comfy on the back seat!

Sheepdogs

It has often been said, that a dog is man's best friend, but to a farmer, a dog is not just a friend, it is part and parcel of his very life, as he simply couldn't manage without one. A good dog saves him many a mile of walking over rough ground, climbing over walls, or round thorn dykes. Whether it is just a case of rounding the sheep up, to be counted, or moving them from one field to another, one can be sure the dog will do ninety percent of the work. Because of this, they had to be well catered for, and were fed with bread, milk, and boiled taties, mixed with meal. There were no tins of Bonio, Pal, or such like, in those days, yet the dogs were always fit and healthy. As for the cats, they had a plentiful supply of milk, but if they fancied a 'meat dish' - they had to catch it first

Our dogs were all the 'cur' type, with names like Laddie, Glen, and Jack, among others, and regarding intelligence, - they couldn't be beaten. Old Jack was a big rough-haired dog, and when in the house, he always lay right behind Dad's chair, to show that he belonged to the boss, and no one else. Dad often tried to play a trick, and sneak out of the house without him, but he never got as far as the back door, till the old dog was on his feet, wagging his tail, and ready for off.

I have many times helped Dad drive a flock of sheep to the local Auction Mart. at Workington, which was three miles away, and have been jolly glad of the dogs help, - sending it forward to guard a gap, or rounding up a stray. I well remember one of these jaunts, when the old dog ran in front of a motor car, on Washington Street, and damaged his back leg. This meant I had to take him back to St Helens on the bus, instead of walking. I picked him up as best I could, and staggered with him to the bus station. The bus being a 'double decker', - I was able to lie him under the stairs. However, when the conductor arrived, I had a fierce argument with him because he wanted to charge me twopence fare, for the dog. I refused point blank pleading that old Jack was a 'hospital case'. We were still arguing the point, when the bus stopped at St Helens, to let me alight, so I carefully lifted the dog off, and laid him by the roadside, until I was able to bring a horse and cart to carry him home to the farm. Only then did I realise that, due to the argument, I hadn't even paid my own bus fare, never mind the dogs! Luckily, old Jack rallied, much to our relief, as he was an excellent working dog.

'Laddie'

Very wise he was too, and showed it every dinnertime. We used a very large enamel pudding dish, to make our daily pudding, either rice, tapioca, or macaroni, and there was nothing Jack liked better than clean out the dish, so we always made sure there was a bit left for him. The funny thing was, Jack kept an eye on the dish throughout the meal, and whenever it moved, so did he. As it got passed round, so the lads could help themselves, Jack followed it, until it was eventually put down on the stone floor for him to enjoy, and with the help of his paws and teeth, he scraped it out as clean as a whistle. After a good wash, the dish was ready for the next day's pudding, and no one gave hygiene a thought!

To see a true shepherd working his flock, with a couple of good dogs, is a sight worth seeing, and must be seen to be believed. Scientists have invented some wonderful things, these past fifty years, even making something capable of travelling to the moon and back, but as for them inventing anything more intelligent than a well-trained sheepdog, that to me, is an impossibility.

A good working dog is worth its weight in gold, and as long as we have shepherds, a dog will not be far behind.

Granda reckoned it took a lazy man, to train a good sheepdog, because he taught it to do much of the work, thus easing his own legs. Now-a-days, agricultural shows, and sheepdog trials are well worth attending, just to see these dogs at work. Like everything else, shepherding has altered over the years, but basic facts remain the same. Shepherds still tend their flocks, but can now often be seen travelling across the field or fell, riding a broad-tyred three wheeled motor bike, instead of walking, so it appears that not only have the sheepdogs got wiser!

Pigs

What could be uglier than a pig? Yet, like everything else on the farm, it was there for a purpose, living in a sty next to the turnip house. It didn't cause a lot of work, and surprisingly, didn't make a lot of noise either, except about eight o'clock in the morning, and half past four in the evening, which were regular feeding times, then it would squeal blue murder until it's trough was filled.

There isn't a great deal to tell about the life of a pig, - all it ever needed, was feeding, with pig meal and boiled potatoes, plus keeping it clean, with plenty of dry straw, and it's sty had to be 'mucked out' weekly, otherwise the smell was past biding. However, one of the busiest days of the year in our farming calendar, was the day we killed the pig, which was an annual ritual.

One often hears soppy stories about other people who have fed, and looked after a pig for twelve months, only to find they had got too fond of it, and hadn't the heart to kill it, because the family couldn't bear the thought of eating poor old Susie, or what ever it's name was. That never happened on our farm! No, we were brought up to know that a pig was there for one reason only, - to provide us with ham and bacon to last twelve months.

One of the main jobs on killing day, was keeping the big set-pot boiling in the wash house, as a never-ending supply of boiling water was needed. A chap called Jack Rule from Seaton, always butched the pig, and was on the job by break of daylight. In our backyard was the slaughter house, the pig sty being directly opposite it, so the animal hadn't far to travel to it's doom, and didn't get a chance to take off, as pigs are apt to do. I never actually witnessed the killing, but I know a "humane killer' was used, and the pig didn't suffer, we also knew that when the squealing stopped, the work started! Bucket after bucket of boiling water was carried from the wash house to the slaughter house, where by now the pig was hanging up by it's back legs, from a low beam, the water being used to mainly scrape the hair off. Blood was kept in a scalded bucket, ready for making the black puddings, and the offal put into a large dish. There was also plenty of fat, in a well-fed pig, this making excellent lard. Then came the job of cutting up the pig, - back legs of course were for the hams, the head was kept for making potted meat, as were the trotters.

Stable Lamp

Spare-rib was cut into sizeable pieces, ready for making delicious tatie pots, and all the scraps of meat were thrown into another clean bucket, later used to make sausages.

Skins needed for the sausages were part of the pig too, all having to be scraped, cleaned, and well washed, before use. A large mincer, kept in the dairy, was used only once annually, - this was to make the sausages. We put the meat, fat, and seasoning through the mincer, making sure it got well mixed, then a long funnel was put in place, and the whole lot was put through the mincer again. As it came out, it was forced into the skin, already stretched over the funnel, and so the sausages were made, to any desired length, some being long, others made into small curly ones, especially for the children. All the farm servants got a piece of spare rib, and a length of sausage to take home, so it was a red-letter day for them.

Black puddings were made the same way using a mixture of blood, barley, cut up fat, warm milk, and a handful of oatmeal. The hams were 'salted down' on slate sconces, behind the dairy door. To do this, we used rough common salt, plus a little ' salt peter', which looked like salt, but was very bitter, obviously containing some sort of chemical, to help the preserving process. The hams lay in brine for seven weeks, being turned at regular intervals, then lifted out, and left twenty four hours to dry, before being rubbed back and front with rough oatmeal. When completely dry, they were wrapped in clean white butter muslin, and hung onto the big hooks suspended from beams in the farmhouse kitchen. These were just within the door, so that fresh air would circulate round them, every time the door opened. Huge sides of bacon were cured the same way, and hung beside the hams.

Pig killing days were hard work, but when we saw all the good food hanging up, knowing it would last us twelve months, it gave us a sense of achievement, and we knew it had been time well spent. Then before many days had past, we had another young pig in the sty, and the rigmarole stated again. Now-a-days few farmers have pig killing days, they are usually sold at auction, and go through the usual channels of slaughter etc. Less work no doubt, but not half as satisfying as having a butcher call, to stage the annual ritual.

Crops

We grew a variety of crops on the farm, especially corn and hay, mainly used for feeding the stock. Cabbage, carrots, turnips and mangolds were grown too, mostly for human consumption, but also fed to the cows. We also grew a large amount of kale, tall green, and leafy, making grand feed when the cattle were 'lying in'. However, our main crop was potatoes, which were grown on many an acre, the chief varieties being King Edwards and Catrionas which were redskins. Only twice a year, did we hire children, one being turnip thinning time, when the rule was "pull out the wrecklings, leaving a hands breadth between the strongest", then again at potato picking time, when the children had a holiday from school for the event.

The old tatie digger had a large iron wheel, with fork-like ends all round it, this wheel rotated, and dug up the potatoes as it went round. They flew in all directions, much to the children's delight, who were paid to pick them up, and put them into sacks. They never made a fortune, probably two shillings; every penny being hard earned. Women came too, and often made it a social occasion, bringing flasks and sandwiches, to last them and the children all day. It was an exceptionally dirty job, if the weather was wet, but this never seemed to deter the families who came, though it was hard work, many a happy day was spent in the fields.

Using a swill to sort 'taties'

Sometimes, the tatie-sorter would be brought onto the job, this being like a huge riddle, spread over a table, where a handle turned on the side, caused the riddle to shake, then the small potoes dropped through, - thus they were sorted. The big ones were laid into long piles, called ‘clamps’, and these were thatched with straw, to keep out the frost. Those not clamped, were sorted in the barn, - small ones to be boiled for the pig, medium ones for seed, and big ones for sale. Plenty had to be kept for our own use, because we used at least a hundredweight per week, in the farmhouse.

Harvest Time

Of all the seasons in the farming year, the hardest, yet the one we enjoyed most, was harvest time, which usually started mid August, and ended late September, or early October, according to the weather. We grew mostly corn, plus the occasional field of wheat, or barley. Harvest time really started at the end of the previous year, when the ploughing was done, before the harrows, discs, and cultivators broke up the soil, in Spring, then rolled, before and after the corn was sown. At this stage, a few scarecrows were set in place, to try and keep the crows and pigeons away, until the seed had a chance to set, otherwise there would be patches of sieves, plus bright red poppies, and no corn. Once the seed started to grow, the field was left to take care of itself, the crop depending on the quality and quantity of the manure used.

While waiting for the corn to mature, we were kept busy in other fields, haytiming, and praying for fine weather, When the hay was being cut, with a Bamford mowing machine, the teeth of the blade had to be kept exceptionally sharp, so two blades were kept available, each with individual teeth, so if one tooth got broken, as often happened, it could easily be replaced, without the whole blade being discarded. After cutting, it was laid in rows, then the hayturner was used, plus the swath turner, wuffler, and side delivery rake, - anything at all, to keep the hay moving, letting air through, to dry it. Eventually, it was put into haycocks, like miniature haystacks. When the hay was completely dry, which again depended on the weather, the lads would be sent to turn the haycocks over, and upside down. This was known as "towpun t'cocks ower", then it was a case of getting the hay inside, this being dealt with in the same way as the harvest described later.

Only after haytime was finished, could we turn our minds back to the harvest, which by now, should be ripe and golden in colour, and if we were lucky, standing straight, though more often than not, quite a lot was flattened by wind and rain. Whatever the case, it had all to be cut, using a McCormick binder, which was a wonderful machine, in those days. A big arm like a windmill swept over it first, to lay the stalks all one way, as the blade cut it, before it travelled on a moving canvas, and into the actual binder, which bound the corn into sheaves, each sheaf being tied round the middle, with a piece of string, before being thrown out of the machine. The special string used was called binder twine, but for some

Haytiming

unknown reason, in our area, it was commonly called 'John Robert'.

While bindering was in progress, chaps from the village brought their lurcher dogs to catch rabbits, when they left the corn, as the binder passed through, - many a fine hare we've had for the pot! These dogs very often got in the path of the binder, and it has been known for them to loose a leg, if the horses couldn't be pulled up fast enough. Two good horses were needed to pull the binder, and hard work it was too. They worked for just two hours, then had a rest, while two others took over, thus they worked in relays. After bindering the sheaves were put into 'stooks', - four leaning against four, to let the air through, so drying the corn. These stooks were left standing a few days, then were "towped ower" to let the stalks dry, before we started ' housing time', - getting the corn back to the homestead.

To do this, we used horses of course, plus at least six block carts, with shelvings on, - these being wooden contraptions, which fit over the cart, and stuck out like a shelf, all round, so we could get a decent load aboard. Some of the loads had to travel over a mile, most of it on a main trunk road, so loading was a specialised job, and not to be undertaken lightly. A certain number of sheaves to be laid one way, then others the opposite way, because if the load was too light over the horse's back, it was apt to tip up, enroute, despite it being tightly roped. If this should happen, there was wigs on the green, because it had to be dealt with on the spot, thus spoiling the 'run' of the loads, which was essential.

While one cart was being loaded, another would be standing by, waiting, so the horse was able to graze. Meanwhile, another cart at the other end of the journey, was being unloaded, and all the other carts were on the road, either loaded or empty, somewhere between the field and home. Half of the men were in the field, and the other half at the farm, while the two youngest lads and myself, were leading the horses between us, keeping things on an even keel. While travelling to and fro, we carried drinks for the workers, the most popular being cold spring water, with a handful of oatmeal thrown in, reckoned to be the best drink for slaking dry throats. Beside this, we carried ten o'clocks, dinner, tea, and often six o'clocks, if working late. These meals usually consisted of thickly cut sandwiches, and a large piece of cake. I can remember one lad hired with us, called Sydney, always ate his cake first "in case I turn a bad fettle before I get to it"!

The only time some of us stopped harvesting, was to milk the cows, deal with the milk, and feed the calves. Otherwise we worked non-stop. I can well remember harvesting the Pinfold field, late into the night, because the weather was good, and the corn was in good fettle. However, when harvest time was over, and the last load was safely home, it was time to celebrate, with a traditional 'Kern supper' which is what most Cumbrian farmers did.

Everyone who had helped, in any way, plus friends and neighbours all turned up, and we never had less than twenty to feed. We always put on a good spread, for the 'do', which meant boiling one of our own hams in the set-pot, to wet the appetite. We also made trays of special teacakes with extra fat in, commonly known as 'funeral biskies', but we stretched a point, and baked them for the Kern supper, because they went down well with the ham, or rum butter, specially made too. Two scalded milking buckets were used to mix the salad, and we ended the meal with blackite (bramble) cake covered with fresh cream. Every one got a glass of homemade burnet wine, as Dad always proposed a toast, to "The next twelve months". The meal was followed by a jolly singsong, complete with accordion, mouth organ, Jew's harp, even comb and greaseproof paper! I thumped out many a grand tune on the old piano, but not before I had lit the candles, in the ornate brass candlesticks, which were hinged, and swung out from front of the piano, thus giving me an extra bit of light. My brother Cyril always sang Egremont Crab Fair, while a chap called Billy Walker was an expert at playing two spoons, by clapping them together, up his arms, down his legs, and over his head - wonderful! I remember Billy Hughes reciting a humorous rhyme entitled "When the Baby Chewed the Brass Knobs off the Fender!"

Nights well worth remembering were these. and it was at this 'do' that many farmers took the last sheaf of corn to be brought from the harvest field, and hung it on a beam in the farmhouse kitchen. This was supposed to guarantee good crops the following year, but Dad never did this, - he always reckoned that nothing but hard work, and good management produced good crops, not a relic of last years labours! Another thing he never liked, was when the local chapel at Rye Hill held it's harvest festival, singing "All is Safely Gathered in" when half of the harvest was still lying out in the field, probably wet and wasted, but if we'd had a good harvest, and all the corn was 'safely gathered in' - nobody enjoyed the harvest festival more than he did, and would sing 'Plough the Fields and Scatter" with the best of them! Again, it is funny how little things stick in the mind, as I remember it was while he and I were walking home across the fields, from the Chapel Harvest Festival, that we usually felt the first nip of frost in the air, and I knew then, that ploughing season lay directly ahead, and the whole process of harvesting was about to start again.

Threshing Day

We never looked upon the harvest season as being finished, until the thresher had paid a visit, - this belonged to old Joe Thompson, of Gilcrux. Threshing day was a day on it's own, and everybody had to be out of bed rather earlier than usual, to get the morning milking done, and stock fed, before we started the threshing. More often than not, the thresher arrived the previous night; we could watch it chugging its way along the road, for a mile before it turned into our farm lane. It was pulled by a big black steam engine, which puffed out black smoke, as it crawled along at an average speed of five miles per hour, with the threshing machine tagged on behind. When it eventually reached the barn where we were planning to thresh, it was backed into place, not without a lot of pulling, chugging, and steaming, it being such a cumbersome piece of machinery. When at last it was in the required position, the engine was stopped allowing it to cool overnight. This was known as having the thresher 'set up' therefore ready for business, so we able to get cracking first thing the following morning.

Two lads stood on top of the cornstack, forking corn onto the thresher top, and one was kept busy with a very sharp knife, cutting the string from round the sheaves, before putting them into the actual machine. This was known as 'feeding the thresher', and after the sheaves had gone through the process, corn, or wheat, as the case may be, poured out of the back of the thresher, and ran into course hessian bags, which held eight stone weight each. These bags were hooked onto a shute, catching the grain as it left the thresher, one lad doing nothing else but keep an eye on them, making sure they didn't over-flow. Woe betide them, if this happened, because old Joe had a tongue that could 'clip cloots' and often used it if he thought any lad wasn't paying attention to his work.

Another lad wheeled the full bags into the near-by barn using a 'sack bogie', while the youngest ones were kept busy moving the straw and chaff, as it left the machine. Most of the chaff was used as bedding for the calves, but when we were children, threshing day was a great occasion for us, because this was the day we emptied the 'chaff beds' we slept on, and refilled them with fresh chaff, straight from the thresher, and what a lovely sweet smell it had! A spare bag was filled too, in case we needed a 'shakky doon' for unexpected visitors. This was a spare bed, hastily made by lying the bag of chaff on the floor, and covering it with a quilt. As children, we loved these 'shakky doons' and willingly gave up our beds to visitors, to use them.

During the threshing, old Joe himself kept steam up and made sure the belt stayed on the pulley, as this was actually making the machine work. Everyone knew their own job, and just got on with it. Chaps from the nearby villages of Siddick and Flimby always turned up with their terriers, to catch the rats as they left the stack. I've known them catch twenty or more, in the day, so there was always plenty of sport, as well as hard work.

Plenty of food was available too, for all who came to help, as we were allowed extra rations from the Food Office, to help cater for the event. Threshing days don't occur now, due to the modern machinery available, harvesting now being completed within days. - often within hours, - what a labour-saving thought! Yet surely some of the 'magic' has been lost? - What, no horses? No towping stooks over? No working by moonlight? No Kern supper? No threshing day? - Modern day farmers don't know what they've missed!

Bait time

Poultry

We had quite a lot of poultry on the farm, mainly Light Sussex and Rhode Island Red hens, along with white Aylesbury ducks. There isn't a lot to tell about the subject, but I take delight in re-telling two humorous tales about poultry, concerning events which happened on our farm. Readers will have no doubt heard the story of "The House That Jack Built". Well here follows a similar tale I shall call "The Hut that Malcolm Built"

Malcolm was my brother who kept a few chickens every Spring, until they were pullets on the point of lay, then sold to make a bit of pocket money. He kept them in an empty pigsty in the farmyard, till one day the space was needed for some piglets, so Malcolm had to build a hut for his chickens. Having no idea at all, how to go about it, he thought up a good idea. Cutting four of the straightest branches he could find, from the apple trees in our orchard, he hammered them down into the ground, at four strategic points, to form a square. He next collected a lot of old wooden boards from a heap in the farmyard, and simply nailed them round the four corner posts. When the structure rose to be five feet high, he nailed some tin sheeting across the top to make a roof.

It looked fine, until he realised it had no door, so he took his saw, and from one of the walls, he sawed a large oblong shaped piece of wood, which immediately fell into short boards as it hit the ground. Quite undaunted, he nailed them together and placed the finished article back into position, where of course, it fit exactly, then used two pieces of old clog leather as hinges, the end result being a perfect door, - what could be simpler? A similar small hole was cut in the side, as a window, this being covered with wire netting held on with staples, as he had no idea how to fix a pane of glass. All that was needed now, was two perches, which were easily erected, then the hut was ready for occupation.

The pullets seemed to like their new abode, having the best of both worlds, as they were allowed free range throughout the orchard. In due course, they were ready for selling, and a chap bought them on condition he could buy the hut too, otherwise he had nowhere to keep them. So the deal was made, and the buyer said he would move them himself, to Clifton, the following day. However, when Malcolm came home from the fields, at the said time, the buyer was waiting, to tell him he had taken the pullets, and had a horse and cart standing by, to take the hut, but had been unable to move it.

Feeding the pullets

On closer examination, it was found that the four 'corner posts' had taken root, and were actually sprouting fresh green leaves! The pullets had been eating these, as they formed. Quite unconcerned, Malcolm once again took up his faithful saw, and sawed through the 'corner posts' at ground level, thus leaving the hut movable. Later, Malcolm said he was quite satisfied with the price he got, but had he known the circumstances, he'd have charged extra for the fresh green salads available to the residents.

"What a bargain"

Another day I did a favour for a neighbour by moving some furniture with my horse and cart, and in return, she gave me ten duck eggs, assuring me they were fertile, if I could find a broody hen to sit them. This I did, and in due course became the proud owner of ten fine khaki - Campbell ducklings. As they matured their feathers took on a lovely glossy sheen, and looked first class, as they swaddled around the farmyard, until one afternoon, a chap by the name of Jack Mossop called, just as I was crossing the yard.

Looking around he said "By gum, - what fine ducks, I could just do with them, to clear all the slugs from my orchard, - they belong to the boss, I suppose?" "Well you suppose wrong" I answered "because they're mine, I wasn't thinking of selling them, but if the price is right, I'll consider it". By trade Jack was a dealer in livestock, and very seldom carried money around, but said "I've just taken two pigs to Lamplugh, and exchanged them for an elderly cow, not in good fettle, - how about swapping it for the ducks?" "Not until I've seen the cow" I answered, so we walked round the corner, to where his motor car and trailer were parked.

I took one look of sheer disbelief - 'You call that a cow?" I joked - " it hasn't enough meat on it to make a decent tatie pot!" It certainly looked as though it was on it's last legs, and well past it's 'sell by date', but Jack continued " I really don't want it, but didn't want to be left with the pigs either, - you can have the cow in exchange for the ten ducks". On the spur of the moment, I said "Yes, I'll risk it" then spent the next ten minutes catching the ducks, which Jack put into his trailer, letting out the apology for a cow. It hadn't enough strength to run away, so I let it wander around until I had time to bother with it.

After Jack had gone, I looked over the poor creature, and immediately, christened it "Miserable Minnie", then put her in a small field, with a stream through, and left her there, quite close to the homestead, and as the weather was warm and sunny, she had nothing to do but recuperate. The old girl steadily improved, slowly putting on weight, until it became obvious she was in calf, - wonders never cease! However, I left her where she was, then one day, much to my delight, I found her suckling a bonny roan heifer calf. They both lay out all summer, then when the colder weather approached I brought them into the farmyard.

I'd just got the cow inside the byre, intending to put the calf in a pen, when who should walk in the yard, but Jack Mossop, and I could sense immediately that he was interested. I deliberately let the calf go 'walk about' so that Jack could see all it's good points, till eventually he said "My! - That's a beauty!" Naturally I agreed with him, not pushing the matter, as I hadn't thought of selling it, but was always open to offers, especially as I'd noticed his trailer was empty. "Fancy it"? I asked, "Aye" answered Jack, still watching the calf, before he asked "How much?" Without hesitation, I said "Seven pounds ten shillings" thinking I could always drop down a bob or two. To cut a long story short, we agreed on a straight five pounds, and as Jack had just been to Broughton Moor, selling a few big lambs, he had five pounds in his pocket, so we struck a deal.

It was only when the money was safely in my pocket, and the calf in the trailer, did I tell him he had paid five pound for a calf which was inside the cow he had swapped for the ducks, therefore he'd paid ten bob for each for the ducks, which he could have bought any Monday at Mitchell's auction for half a crown each! Being the good-hearted fellow he was, he took it all in good part, saying, " I thought I was a good dealer, but you'll make a better".

Yes, I felt I'd got a good deal, because after all I still had 'Miserable Minnie' in the byre.

Still on the subject of poultry, - Every Spring, a chap called Fred Cunliffe, who lived at Flimby, set some goose eggs, and hatched out a dozen goslings. These he reared until they were about ten weeks old, then they came to St Helens, and were housed in the orchard, until it was time to fatten them for Christmas, when they were kept indoors. Every morning, the geese were let out into the open field, next to the orchard, and it was my job to herd them back in, at night, keeping them safe from the local fox, who had a lair in nearby Aigle Ghyll woods. As the geese often wandered, I took Laddie, our sheepdog with me on these occasions, and he soon learnt to round them up. While strolling home behind the geese each night, I practised playing the mouth organ, which I carried permanently in the pocket of my 'bib and brace' overalls, so the geese were serenaded with anything from Daisy Bell to the Blue Danube, to accompany them back to the orchard.

On the very odd occasion I wasn't available to 'put the flock to bed', one of the lads did the job for me, but always reckoned they were difficult to herd, and took time to settle, so no doubt they missed their evening lullaby.

Incidentally - I offered to teach the lad how to play the mouth organ, but he reckoned if he managed that, he might get the job of herding the geese every night, so wasn't risking it, - wise lad!

Visitors

Though we lived a distance from the nearest village, we were never short of visitors, one being Pat Cameron, the local "Gentleman of the Road" who, for some obscure reason, sported a black bowler hat, along with his raggy outfits. Pat called regularly, every third week, and was always given a buttered teacake and a threepenny piece, for which we got a muttered "Ta". However, after one of his visits, my sister happened to go into the orchard for firewood, and what did she find? - The buttered teacake still in it's paper bag, which had been thrown over the wall, from the lane leaving the farm. Obviously, Pat hadn't been hungry, and didn't think the teacake worth carrying till the next mealtime. Needless to say, - next time he called he got 'short shrift' no teacake, and no threepenny piece!

Some salesmen called weekly, including Mr Pickering the chemist from Maryport, selling medicines for both humans and animals, Mr Rennick travelled for "Bowe and Clark" a firm of drapers from Cockermouth, Firns the ironmongers also came from Cockermouth, and from them, we bought "Clover leaf' sile pads for the milk cooler. 'Oily Johnny" brought paraffin, on a pony-drawn flat cart, from the back end of which he sold fruit! Geordie Greenhow the local butcher called twice weekly. Each Friday, we bought the weekend joint, which had to be a big one, as it needed to feed at least twelve of us. There was always enough left to make a tatie pot on Mondays, yet the weekly meat bill was never more than two pound.

A lady carrying a 'pack' called at the farm on a monthly basis, travelling by bus, before carrying her load up the farm lane. Her 'pack' consisted of various lengths of material, towels, and the odd shirt, I don't know her real name, but she was always known as 'Nanny Berry'. She had her dinner with us, and while doing so, told us some very interesting tales about the 'travelling folk', which fascinated me, and I looked forward to her visits. "Darkie Joe" called too, carrying his wares in a large brown suitcase, from which he sold a manner of oddments. Even during the Second World War, when such necessities as knicker elastic was unobtainable in the shops, it could always be purchased from the bottom of Darkie Joe's case, along with other 'hard to get' articles. My younger sister was frightened of him, and always made herself scarce when he was around. She wasn't too keen on the two gypsies either, who sold home-made clothes pegs, and offered to fore-tell our future, if we "crossed their palms with silver". Dad didn't believe in this, - his philosophy on life being 'work or want' and as far as the future was concerned, - 'wait and see'.

Another interesting caller was the man who made tins, and visited us every six months. These tins were of a very high quality, including cake tins, bread tins, pie tins and roasting tins. We could hear him coming at a distance, as he had all the tins slung round his neck on a rope, and they jangled, every step he took. One visitor who was actually a customer, arrived at the farm early every Friday morning, after walking from Flimby. To this day, I don't know his proper name, as we always called him 'The sixpenny man" this was because each time he came, he handed over a sixpenny piece, and in return, he expected (and got) enough vegetables to last him and his family a full week, - a turnip, some carrots, and a 'scowp' full of taties.

Old Gosh Crellin, a man with a long white beard, got a bag full of vegetables too, and we didn't even get sixpence for them. He delivered our Sunday newspapers (which came by bus, to the bottom of the lane, during the week). When we paid him for the papers. Dad also gave him the vegetables, by the way of saying 'Thankyou' for walking from Flimby, in all weathers. He was a real character, and always made a point of telling us, if even one of last week's taties was 'a baddun'. Gosh was a real storyteller, and I enjoyed hearing him tell the tale about his furniture when he first got married. He reckoned that he and his wife had only two orange boxes between them, to start off their married life, so they sat on one, when eating a meal, and used the other as a table, then when night time drew nigh, they put them both together, and used them as a bed, to sleep on.

Nicholas Tenby was the man who delivered the Parish Magazine from St Nicholas Church at Flimby, every month, but if there were any cows, or sheep, in the farmyard, he wouldn't come near, so left the magazine tucked in the sneck of the orchard gate. If the wind blew it away, before we retrieved it, that was just our hard luck.

Among the 'regulars' who came daily, for milk, was an old loveable rogue called Flek, and Dad used to say of him, "There is only one thing old Flek won't pinch, - that's something he can't lift". Others, who came for milk, were Mrs Hewitt, Mrs Moore, and Mrs Stephenson, all carrying tin cans with lids on. Two other visitors were Maggie Moon, who collected a weekly penny for the "Local Forces Comforts Fund" and Esther Banton, who also collected one penny per week from us, and this entitled the whole family to the services of the local District Nurse, when necessary.

Looking back, we certainly had a mixed variety of callers, one of the most colourful being the "Mowdy Man" who came in Spring, to trap moles which were very plentiful. As he caught, and killed them, he tied each one by it's tail, to the nearest fence, for all to see. This was to prove he was worthy of his hire, and was paid the princely sum of twopence per mole, plus his dinner of course. Another regular diner at our table, was "Swilley Allen" the chap who made swills, usually from strips of willow. These were large flat baskets, with two 'hand holes', and very useful things they were, for carrying taties, turnips, or meal etc. Swilley had regular customers for his wares, who were always glad to buy from him.

Two lads worthy of a mention, were the Scott brothers, who came from a very poor family, and visited us every evening, hoping to get at the very least, a drink of fresh warm milk, straight from the cow. One summer, two of our cows developed ringworm, - a very contagious ailment, quite common, when we were farming. These two boys spent a full evening, rubbing their bare backs against the infected animals, hoping to 'catch' the ringworm, so they would not be able to go school. When Dad found out about the episode, he chased them off the premises, and banned their return for a month.

Not every visitor was welcome, - there was one particular chap who came every week, and I didn't like him, because he was always complaining. One day, I sold him a stone of carrots, and when I handed him the bag, he argued he hadn't been given full weight, so I weighed the goods again, to prove he had, then sent him packing, still complaining. Later the same day, he arrived back, demanding to see Dad. Apparently, I had accidentally dropped the half stone weight off the weighing machine, into his bag, so he had just half a stone of carrots, plus the half-stone weight, which I was glad to have back. He was not amused, when I apologised briefly, before pointing out to him that he needn't have carried all the carrots back to the farm, - the half-stone weight was proof enough!

Lastly, I must not forget to mention the Prudential Insurance man, who walked up the farm lane one dark night, and swore a ghost had jumped out of the dyke, and frightened him. Because of this, he refused to go back alone, so Dad had to go with him, and found that the 'ghost' was a white leghorn clocker, sitting on eggs. It had obviously been disturbed, probably by a cat, and had flown from the nest, just as the 'man from the Pru' happened to be passing. Speaking of ghosts, the following chapter consists of two true stories, describing 'happenings' on two different Halloween nights.

Halloween

Halloween night was one of the highlights of our year, as we had a special supper to celebrate the event, consisting of as much 'Spotted Dick' pudding as we could eat. This Roly Poly suet pudding, was boiled for two hours, in a very large oval pan, on the fire grate in the washhouse. Custard was made by suspending a scalded bucket, full of milk, from a pole laid across the brim of the big set pot (boiler) which was half filled with boiling water. When the milk in the bucket began to boil, the custard powder and sugar were stirred in, and hey-presto! - We had a bucket of thick creamy custard to serve with the "Spotted Dick' which was always appreciated by everyone, on a chilly October night. After this, no-one felt like moving far, so we erected draught screens round a roaring log fire, and all the younger ones enjoyed a game of snatch apple, then we sat in the lamplight, telling stories which was a regular pastime.

One such night, when I was just a child, old Ike was telling a tale about a witch with a wooden leg, who flew around on her broomstick, looking for youngsters still downstairs, when it was long past their bedtime, and approaching the 'Witching Hour'. Just as Ike finished the tale we heard it, - a distinct tap, tap, tap, and I jumped up onto Dad's knee, putting my arms around his neck. All was quiet for a few minutes, then it came again, - tap, tap, tap. I clung to Dad, as our dog under the sofa started to growl, and two cats sitting on the fender stool arched their backs and began to hiss. My younger sister and I were sure it was the witch walking across the roof of our house, and expected her to float down our wide chimney at any minute.

There it came again, tat, tap, tap, but this time, the taps were followed by a very noisy bang, bang, bang, on the kitchen door. We knew it must be a stranger, because anyone known to us, would have walked straight in, Dad put me down on his chair, and walked towards the door, Rene and I fully expecting to be snatched away, at any minute. However, the door opened to reveal the local tramp, Pat Cameron, complete with his customary black bowler hat. Apparently, he had been enjoying a night's free kip, in the fodder-gang, at the end of the warm byre, when he was woken by the sound of a cow calving. Thinking the cow to be in distress, he thought it best to contact Dad, so was making his way to the kitchen door.

Being pitch dark, he was following the wall of the house, by tapping with his kebby stick, as he slowly found his way over the cobble stones, hence the tapping we had heard. The outcome was. Pat was invited in, to eat up the remains of the "Spotted Dick" while Rene and I went willingly to bed, having heard enough stories to frighten us, for the next twelve months!

"A load of old whitewash!"

When sitting in our farmhouse kitchen, it was easy to conjure up all sorts of things connected with Halloween, because the place was riddled with flying bats, creeping spiders in sticky webs, and slinky black cats with staring yellow eyes. Easy to imagine a few witches with broomsticks, - we even had a real ghost living in our Dutch Barn, who only put in an appearance at Halloween, which was a time for story telling.

I remember one such night, when we all got a good laugh. It so happened, we had a new young lad called Jackie, working for us, a timid lad he was, almost frightened of his own shadow. The other lads had been tormenting him, about our resident ghost, to such an extent, - he was almost too frightened to go upstairs! The lads were pulling his leg about this, when Jackie suddenly stated aloud "Ah'm flate uf nowt!" This encouraged one of the other lads, Ernie, to say, "I'll bet you daren't go through the farmyard tonight, at midnight, walk round the midden, then walk back again". Jackie was trying his hardest to be tough, so he said "Oh yis, I dare do that, - ah'll gaa noo, reet uway" but Ernie said "No, wait till midnight, 'cos that's when t'ghost does his high jinks, if you meet it, just doff your hat, and walk on".

By now, Jackie's eyes were like windmills, but still vowed he would go. Before long, the Grandfather clock struck midnight, - twelve loud ominous strokes, - the witching hour had arrived! Every stroke sounded like a death knell to young Jackie, as he got to his feet, and walked straight out of the door. Ernie followed him, to the farmyard gate, then shouted after him "Bring back the gripe (a three pronged fork) from the midden, then we'll know you've really been that far". He then laughed, and went back into the farmhouse.

Meanwhile, Jackie walked straight on, past the barn as fast as his knocking knees would allow, not daring to glance either right or left, as he scuttered onto the midden, grabbed the gripe, and then turned to retrieve his steps. Suddenly it happened! - His courage failed him, and he stood there, rooted to the spot, not daring to move, either one way or the other. Short of screaming for help, it appeared he would have to stand there till daylight. Then right of the blue, he had a brainwave, - he could get back to the farmhouse, where he wanted to be, without going anywhere near the barn, if he went through the calf pens, over the turnip heap, along the middle byre and out by the fodder-gang. What could be easier? Why hadn't he thought of this before?

So, with a better heart, he set off, - no bother getting through the calf pens, or over the turnip heap, but while making his way along the middle byre, disaster struck! Some of the other lads had been white-washing the byre walls that day, and left their 'gear' handy, ready to start work again next morning. Being in such a hurry, he never saw the old tin bath, full of white-wash, standing in the gangway, and fell right into it, head first, feet last.

When he eventually got scraffled out, he was snow white from top to bottom, and gasping, so the only thing he could do, was to sit down on one of the milking 'coppies' until he got his breath back. He couldn't do anything about his sodden clothes, and it was far too cold to strip them off, so he just picked up his gripe, and set off to walk back to the house.

Meanwhile, all the other lads were wondering what had happened to Jackie. Time went on, and when he didn't show up, Dad said it was up to Ernie to go and look for him, because it was he who had dared him to go to the midden. However, Ernie wasn't as cock-sure of himself, as he made out he was, and the very thought of there being a ghost terrified him, but he had no option but to set off, whistling 'Danny Boy' to give him a bit of Dutch courage.

He opened the yard gate, and was halfway to the midden, when the middle byre door burst open, and out strides this 'departed spirit', not only deathly white, but brandishing a three pronged fork, just like the devil, and at that very same minute, a big white owl flew past, letting out a screech fit to waken the dead. Seeing this white 'spirit' and hearing the blood-curdling scream at the same time, was more than enough for Ernie. He never even saw the five barred gate he leapt over, and was half way to Camerton, before he dare look over his shoulder, to make sure there was nothing frightening following him. Back in the farmyard, Jackie realised what had happened, and knew the shoe was on the other foot now, because he was the one not frightened! As a matter of fact, since then, he's often boasted about being the first ghost to wear a pair of iron-caulkered clogs!

The Farm Sale

In 1947, when St Helen's Farm was sold, the family had to move out, but before we left, we had a traditional farm sale of stock and implements to deal with. Everything to be sold, was laid out in the croft field, except the animals which were kept inside. A very large crowd of farmers and would-be buyers was expected, so we baked ten extra loaves, and boiled a ham, ready to make free sandwiches, which were expected to be provided on sale day. All was made ready the night before, - the parlour being turned into a temporary office, ready for the clerk. The auctioneer was to be Eddie Barwise, a man known in the locality. Everyone worked hard, preparing the sale, and would be glad to see it over.

However, when morning came, a big surprise awaited us, - there had been a heavy fall of snow during the night, - an unheard of thing, in our area. The croft was like a white blanket, with no implements visible at all, except a few pairs of shafts sticking up in the air. After much discussion (and cursing) the decision was made, to cancel the sale, so we were back to square one. We very quickly wrapped the ham in butter muslin, and laid it on a large cold slate in the dairy, knowing it would take no harm until the following week, when the reorganised sale would be held, as we were sure the snow would have melted by then.

However, instead of melting snow, we got a spell of hard frost, lasting until the following Thursday, with a bit of snow melting on the Friday, But many outlying farms were still weather-bound, and we got a very poor turn out, for the Saturday sale, - only about a hundred. There was still a lot of snow around, which meant some of the implements, and smaller articles had to be dug out, before being put on show, ready for inspection by prospective buyers.

Our village policeman at that time, was a chap called Dick Thornborough, who took off his tunic jacket, rolled up his sleeves and sliced ten new loaves baked for the occasion, then sliced the ham, as we made piles of 'doorstep' sandwiches which quickly disappeared during the course of the day. I didn't see many things sold, as I was kept busy otherwise, but I remember Dad saying it had been a 'fair to middling' sale, with the best cows making up to twenty pounds.

It was the list of miscellaneous articles, which fascinated me, when I saw them listed in the sales book, later in the day Two tin buckets were sold at fivepence each, a large bag of mixed nails sixpence, two axes, ninepence, four small hooks, a halfpenny, and six good swills made only one shilling and sixpence. This didn't bother me at all but I know I shed a tear when our lovely big horses left the yard for the last time, and I remember hoping that the buyer would be as kind to them as we had been. However, there wasn't time for regrets, as a new life lay ahead of us, and after the farm was sold, we prepared to move to new pastures making sure we took the dogs with us!

Uncle Willie with block cart

A New Experience

We left St Helens on the second day of February 1947 while the snow still lay on the ground. In those days, this was the customary date for all farmers who were changing farms, to move. Our 'new' farm was called "Buildings Farm" in Lowca Lane, at Seaton, and being only two miles as the crow flies, from St Helens, we knew the area well, before we took up residence. One of the things we missed, was our 'team' of lads for the regular game of Pitch and Toss which we had played every dinner time. This old country sport entailed throwing worn-out horseshoes, from a distance, to hit a target, and in our case, this was the pole on which the dovecote perched. The winner was the person who managed to circle the post with their horseshoe, the game being a great favourite with us all.

One thing that didn't change, was the luck-penny system. If Dad bought a cow, a horse, or even a few sheep, he would pay the agreed price, then expect a small amount of money being given back to him, to wish him luck with his new stock. This was called a 'luck penny' and could range from a ten shilling note, down to a two bob bit, according to the generosity of the seller, and depending on whether he thought he'd had a good deal or not. Similarly, if Dad sold any stock, he would be expected

Ethel on the milk round

to give a 'luck penny' to the buyer. This was a very old Cumbrian custom, practised during and before my Grandfather's farming days, in the early 1900's.

Within days, we had got used to the much smaller farm, which provided work for just four of us, - Dad, sister Kitty, brother Malcolm, and myself. The farm was run on similar lines to St Helen's, but with one big difference, - we had a milk round to contend with, which we'd never experienced before. By now, I was twenty years of age, and was allocated the job of delivering milk to approx. two hundred houses in the village each morning, plus twenty each evening, and I loved every minute of it, finding it a good way to get to know people. The cows were milked twice daily, and because we now had an electricity supply, we had no need to milk by hand, though it took us quite some time to get used with the machine. After cooling the milk, it was put in a milk churn, and loaded onto a small, flat, four-wheeled lorry, drawn by my black and white pony 'Spotty'. The first few weeks, I delivered milk straight into my customer's jugs, by means of a pint and gill measure, hung on the side of the churn. This was very time consuming, so Dad thought we should try the bottle system, which was much easier while on the round, but meant more work at home, as the bottles had to be filled by hand, sealed with a cardboard top, and sterilised every day.

My pony very quickly learnt where to stop, while on the round, and didn't mind leaving me behind, if he thought there would be a crust waiting at the next stop! Prices varied. as the milk was twopence halfpenny per pint, but children under five years of age, and expectant mothers were allowed one pint daily at the cheaper rate of three halfpence, so the 'milk lass' was usually the first to know when a new baby was expected, as I was presented with a green card as proof, but more often than not, I was sworn to secrecy, until the matter became obvious.

I met a lot of very kind people, while delivering milk, and two outstanding characters deserve special mention, though both have long since passed away. One was an elderly man called Willie Houseman, a bachelor, who had a long association with the scouting movement, being the proud owner of many awards, including the Silver Cross for gallantry and the Medal of Merit. He was also an astronomer of note, having an observatory built in his garden, and was a director of the British

Astronomical Association. Mr Houseman could forecast the weather with uncanny accuracy, but despite all his attributes, he was to me, just the friendly genial customer who, when he handed over one shilling and fivepence halfpenny, to pay his weekly milk bill, every Saturday morning, never failed to give me two black mint ball sweets, to "see me on my way". Another elderly customer was called Ann Nixon, and she was the 'hatched, matched and despatched', lady of the village, - present at most births, served at many a wedding feast, but was best known for being the 'layer out' when anyone died. This entailed washing the deceased, and 'laying them out' on the bed, dressed in a long white gown and stockings, amid the best bedding available, always white in colour usually embroidered, or edged with crochet lace. Only after this was done, were the neighbours allowed in, for the 'viewing'. There was nothing Ann liked better, than to describe her latest 'departed' to me, when I called weekly. She would stand and rattle the coins in her hand, but not offer to hand them over until I'd been told every detail, so I had no option but to stand and listen. A lovely natured person, Ann would do a good turn for anyone.

Other customers I well remember, were Will Wright the village dancing master, Danny Casson, the clogger with a twisted leg, who could carry on a conversation whilst holding half a dozen 'sprigs' between his lips, and Harry Blackburn the local newspaper reporter, who could sniff out a story, long before the event happened! These characters, and many more like them, made life 'colourful' to say the least, while delivering the milk.

The various odd questions I was asked by my customers, included "Why has my pot plant died?" "Will six ounces of wool knit our Jack a pullover?" "Why was the doctor at Mrs Smiths late last night?" Is this gingerbread cooked far enough?" Plus the one I was asked on a regular basis - " Can you lend me a penny for the gas meter, otherwise the kids won't get any breakfast?" Every week I collected a parcel of dirty washing from an old lady, and delivered it to her daughter, at the other end of the village, then carried the washed and ironed clothes back to 'Mother' at the weekend. Such was life, working on a milk round, and as I've said, - I loved every minute.

Meanwhile, back on the farm, - life was again ruled by routine, every task having it's allotted time. Even the day I was married, - I felt the wedding was just something to be slotted in, between milking times. At ten o'clock, I was in the middle of the village with my pony and cart, delivering the milk, in the pouring rain, and at eleven o'clock I was standing at the altar, complete with wreath and veil!

One dear old lady kindly asked me if I hadn't thought of delivering the milk the previous evening, thus saving time. This would have proved 'tricky' to say the least, as we had to milk the cows that morning, before I could set off. If I'd asked the cows to perform twice the previous evening because we had a wedding in the offing, - I don't think they'd have been impressed. After the wedding, while travelling by taxi, to the reception, the Milk Marketing Board tanker blocked our way, while the driver alighted, to give us his good wishes, as we knew him well, but I don't think the traffic held up behind him, appreciated the fact. Anyhow, despite all the hiccups, Rev. Johnstone must have tied the knot well, as we have now passed our fiftieth anniversary, and are still friends!

Looking Back

Times change, as the years go by, and nothing has changed more dramatically over the past years, than farming. Years ago, a chap could call himself a farmer, if he had a wheelbarrow, a few Rhode Island hens, a couple of Khaki-Campbell ducks, and an ewe with two lambs in the orchard. All he required in the tool and implement line, were a decent bill-hook and a gripe. Anything else needed, was borrowed from a neighbouring farmer, in return for labour, until he could afford to buy the necessities, because every aspect of farming then, depended on the weather, whether it was ploughing, haytime, harvest, or potato picking etc. But the weather doesn't matter so much now-a-days, because of all the modern machinery that exists.

During his latter years, my Granda was heard to say "If a would-be farmer can afford to buy all the machinery and gadgets reckoned to be 'essential's' to farming today, he could afford to retire before he starts, and save himself a lot of hard work and worry"

Even the farmers themselves have changed, A few years ago, you could always pick out a farmer in a crowd, by his ruddy complexion, corduroy britches, coarse woollen jacket, polished leather leggings, and his kebby walking stick. Now, ninety per cent of them dress in denim ''jeans' 'and quilted anoraks, and don't even look as though they belong to the farming community at all.

I left the farming world behind, in 1951, by which time, I was married, and had a baby son. Shortly after this Dad retired, but because I still live in the same area, I have been able to note drastic changes, especially when I visited our old farm at St Helens, which is almost beyond recognition. Many of the fields are now covered with factories, namely Iggesund Paper Board Mill, Eastman Chemicals, The New Balance Shoe Factory, and Thomas Armstrong Ltd. This of course meant much less land to be cultivated. Gone were all the horses, modern tractors having taken their place, no block carts either, just trailers for the tractors.

It didn't look the same place, but one thing that hasn't altered, was the dry stone walls, which my Granda had built, many years ago, they were standing as erect as ever. He was an expert at building them, and reckoned that a well built dry-stone wall, was as effective as any building, and the animals certainly made use of them, to shelter behind, when the cold winds and rain swept in from the Solway Firth.

St Helens farmhouse is greatly altered too, mainly due to the installed electricity, - a modern cooker instead of the polished grate and fender, and a television set, replacing the old Cosser Radio, with it's dry battery, and accumulator. Gone was the friendly glow of the oil lamps I'd trimmed so often, but did I detect that a lot of the homely atmosphere had gone too? Maybe it is because I am growing older, and one of my pastimes is looking back. Farming in the old days was what I would call real 'down to earth' farming, where as now, it is more like a mechanised, computerised, industry, and I feel that agriculture has lost it's soul.

In our village of Seaton, over the past fifty years, no less than twenty-two farms and smallholdings have ceased to be in existence. Much of the land has given way to housing development, and other fields 'taken over' by larger farms. When all the smallholdings were in full swing, it was customary for the wife to do most of the work, as the husband was usually in full time employment, as a collier or steel worker, and just

St. Helens Farm

‘farmed’ mainly at the weekends. Never the less, - they were part and parcel of the farming community, and it was sad to see their way of life disappear from our area.

Another disturbing feature, not only in our own village, but in the whole County of Cumbria, is the way a lot of barns are being transformed into eye-catching top class houses, which prompts me to ask this question - “What will happen to our lovely barn-owls, - where will they nest, in years to come?”

Many years ago, a chap called William Blake wrote a song, about England’s green and pleasant land. Somehow or other, I feel he must have had farming connections, and I believe that at some future date, the wheel will have turned full circle, and industry will run out of oil and electricity, and then, the old-fashioned farmer, with his small holding and wheelbarrow, will make a come-back. If this should happen, let us hope there is still a little bit of England’s green and pleasant land left, to welcome him, and we may yet again hear him sing -

“To plough, to sow,
To reap and mow,
To be a farmer’s boy!”

"What of the Future?'

What lies ahead, for farmers?
- we cannot know the score,
Life will never ever be
As it was before,
We always milked the dairy cows
By hand sat on a stool,
Now, this is out-dated
- automation is the rule,
We cooled the milk by water
And sold it fresh each day,
Now, it's sterilised and pasteurised
And traumatised I'd say.
We made our own farm butter
With nothing else but cream'
Now, it's full of 'additives'
And microbes, it would seem.
We bought meat from the butcher
- two pounds was all we spent,
Now pre-packed in plastic,
it's "Robbery with intent"
We used to love a "Spotted Dick"
With custard made to pour,
Now, it's foreign pizzas
From the super-market store,
We used to have an oven,
and black-lead polished grate,
Now we microwave our food
Before it's 'sell by' date.
We always used the horses
To plough, and pull the cart
Now, there's modern tractors
Needing diesel oil, to start.
We gathered all the corn sheaves
And 'stooked' them cock-a-hoop
Now, the combine harvester
Does all, in one fell swoop,
We bought our shirts and towels
From the lady with a pack,
Now we buy from catalogues

Or Marks and Spencers rack.
We always used a stable lamp
To show a bedtime light,
Now we press a tiny switch
Hey Presto! - all is bright
We used to feed our sheepdogs
With taties, milk, and meat,
Now it's Pal, Bounce and Bonio
With choc-drops for a treat.
We always got an invoice
And paid our bills with cash,
Now it's W.W.dot com,
And forward slash

Times are changing swiftly
years are but a number,
They choose to call it progress
Which really makes me wonder -
What is going to happen,
In future years ahead,
Will farmers be redundant
And robots farm, instead?
Will real food be abolished
- replaced with sugared pill,
When all crops are organic,
will it be for good, or ill?
Will future generations
Ever see a field of corn,
Hear the plaintive bleat of lambs
On Springtime's early morn?
Will farming as we knew it
Be ever seen again
When harvest-time depended
On sunshine, and the rain?
I look towards the future,
And here's what I fore-see
N.F.U. rules parliament
While farmers plough the sea.
Rockets replace the tractors,
Food falls from the sky,
Pills for tea, farms rent free,
And who knows, - pigs may fly!